Williams J Rollins

RIO DE JANEIRO TRAVEL GUIDE 2023

*Discover Secret Treasures, Gorgeous Beaches, Wildlife
&Waterfalls with our Ultimate Guide for First-Time Visitors.*

First edition

Contents

1.

    1.

        2.

        3.

        4.

        5.

        6.

        7.

2.

1.
  2.
  3.
  4.
  5.
  6.
  7.
  8.
  9.
  10.
  11.
  12.
3.
  1.
    2.
    3.
    4.
    5.
4.
  1.
    2.
    3.
    4.
    5.

6.

5.

   1.

6.

   1.

      2.

      3.

      4.

      5.

      6.

      7.

      8.

7.

   1.

      2.

      3.

      4.

      5.

      6.

      7.

      8.

      9.

      10.

      11.

8.
    1.
9.
    1.
10.
    1.
11.
    1.
12.
    1.
13.
    1.

Chapter 1

INTRODUCTION TO THE MARVELOUS CITY

Rio de Janeiro, the "Marvelous City," welcomes you! Rio de Janeiro, one of the world's most beautiful cities and a popular destination for visitors from all over the globe, is a bustling metropolis rich in culture, history, and natural beauty.

This gorgeous city in Brazil's southeastern area is home to some of the world's most recognizable sites and attractions, including the world-famous Christ the Redeemer statue, the picturesque Copacabana beach, and the unusual Sugar loaf Mountain.

The city is known for its breathtaking natural beauty, which you can see for yourself by riding the cable car to the summit of Sugarloaf Mountain or visiting the lush rainforest of Tijuca National Park.

Rio is also recognized for its active nightlife and vivid culture, as seen by its many bars, restaurants, and nightclubs. Brazilian music, dancing, and culture can all be experienced personally here.

No trip to Rio de Janeiro would be complete without seeing some of the city's most iconic sites, including the Palace of Fine Arts, the Metropolitan Cathedral, and the Sambódromo, which hosts the city's world-famous Carnival festival.

Rio de Janeiro has something for everyone, from its beautiful beaches to its vibrant nightlife. Rio de Janeiro offers something for everyone, whether you want to go on an adventure, learn about the city's culture, or just relax and enjoy the surroundings.

My Experience in Rio de Janeiro

I recently had the pleasure of visiting Rio de Janeiro, Brazil, and it was nothing short of spectacular. I was taken away by the city's splendor from the time I arrived, with its gorgeous mountainous background, crystal clear waterways, and brilliant white sand beaches.

The vivid culture of the city, with its bustling street performers, bright murals, and broad selection of eateries and bars, was the first thing I noticed. I got the opportunity to sample some of the greatest cuisine and beverages the city has to offer, ranging from classic Brazilian delicacies to current fusion tastes.

I was captivated by the city's famed attractions, such as the iconic Christ the Redeemer monument and the majestic Sugar loaf Mountain, as I explored it. I also got the chance to visit the world-famous beaches of Copacabana and Ipanema, where I basked in the sun and enjoyed the refreshing sea air.

My favorite aspect of the trip, though, was probably my visit to the favelas, where I gained a unique insight into the life of the residents. The close-knit communities, with their strong feeling of pride and togetherness, immediately captivated me.

I was particularly struck by the people's tenacity, who, while living in poverty, had grins on their cheeks and a zest for life.

My journey to Rio de Janeiro was genuinely remarkable, and I eagerly await my return. I would strongly advise anybody searching for an engaging and culturally enlightening experience to pay a visit.

Historical Background

Rio de Janeiro is a bustling and picturesque Brazilian city noted for its spectacular beaches and year-round pleasant weather. With a population of about 6.3 million people, it is the country's second biggest metropolis. Rio de Janeiro has a lengthy and intriguing history that dates back to 1565.

Rio de Janeiro was established in 1565 by the Portuguese navigator Gaspar de Lemos, who landed in Guanabara Bay. The city was founded as a military outpost to safeguard the Portuguese territory in Brazil against French, English, and Dutch incursions and was originally called So Sebastio do Rio de Janeiro.

Rio de Janeiro grew into a busy port city throughout the ages, serving as Brazil's greatest port and the entrance to its colonies in Africa, India, and the East Indies.

It was a significant slave trading hub, and its economy flourished fast as a result of the profitable sugar, coffee, and diamond markets.

Rio de Janeiro had become the capital of Brazil by the nineteenth century, and the city had enjoyed a period of rapid expansion and development. The city hosted the first Olympic Games in South America in 1916 and has remained an important cultural hub.

Rio de Janeiro became a popular tourist destination in the twentieth century as a result of its beautiful beaches, active nightlife, and rich cultural history. There has been considerable achievement in recent years in improving the city's infrastructure and reducing poverty in the region.

Rio de Janeiro is now one of the world's most popular tourist attractions, as well as a major hub for commerce, culture, and entertainment.

The people

Rio de Janeiro is a bustling and diversified metropolis with millions of residents from all walks of life. Rio's residents come from all over the globe, from the city's poorest parts' favelas to the wealthy suburbs and coastal villages.

Rio de Janeiro has a long history of immigration, with individuals from all over the globe bringing with them their cultures, languages, and traditions. The population is made up of several various nationalities, including Africans, Europeans, Middle Easterners, and Asians, as well as a sizable Indigenous Brazilian community.

Rio's residents are noted for their passion for life, as well as their enjoyment of music, dancing, cuisine, and festivals. Carnival is an annual highlight, with thousands of people coming to the streets to celebrate.

Rio also has a vibrant business community, with many small enterprises, entrepreneurs, and start-ups making their mark. The economy of Rio de Janeiro is mostly driven by tourism, although it also has a significant manufacturing and industrial sector.

Rio de Janeiro residents are kind and inviting. They are proud of their city and its many attractions, and they are always eager to share their culture with guests. From the magnificent beaches of Copacabana and Ipanema to the renowned Christ the Redeemer monument and the vibrant street art, the people of Rio will make your vacation unforgettable.

The Culture

Rio de Janeiro is well-known for its lively culture and one-of-a-kind style of life. It has a rich history of cultural influences from indigenous peoples as well as immigrants who have arrived to the city throughout the years. This has resulted in a one-of-a-kind melting pot of culture and customs that can still be found in the city today.

Rio de Janeiro's traditional music, known as "samba," is a blend of African, Portuguese, and indigenous rhythms. It's a kind of music that's often connected with Carnival and the city's thriving nightlife. Rio is also recognized for its traditional dance, particularly samba and frevo.

During the year, the city also hosts a wide variety of cultural activities and events. There are various events that commemorate the city's culture and history, such as the Festival do Rio. The city is also home to the world-renowned Carnival, a festival of music, dancing, and culture.

Rio de Janeiro is equally well-known for its cuisine. The city's restaurants range from traditional Brazilian meal to trendy fusion cuisine. Guests may sample international cuisine as well as traditional Brazilian specialties such as feijoada and acarajé.

Rio is also well-known for its art and architecture. Many art galleries and museums, including the Museum of Modern Art, the National Museum of Fine Arts, and the Museum of Latin American Art, can be found in the city.

There are also other notable architectural monuments, like the Christ the Redeemer statue and the Maracan Stadium.

Rio de Janeiro is a vibrant city brimming with culture, and it's simple to understand why it's one of the world's most popular tourist destinations. From its traditional culture to its contemporary art and architecture, it provides something for everyone. Rio de Janeiro offers it all: a busy nightlife, amazing cuisine, and a one-of-a-kind cultural experience.

Way of life

Rio de Janeiro is well-known for its bright and exuberant way of life. Rio de Janeiro residents love the city's laid-back vibe and soak in its sunny beaches, lively nightlife, and unique cultural experiences.

The city's music and food reflect a distinct combination of African, European, and Brazilian influences. People celebrate their rich history and spend time together in the city's many public squares, parks, and plazas.

Rio de Janeiro residents also enjoy the city's diversified and bustling nightlife. When it comes to having a good time in Rio, there is something for everyone, from samba clubs and bustling pubs to live music concerts.

Rio de Janeiro also hosts many world-class athletic events. Rio de Janeiro attracts sports lovers from all over the globe, from the yearly Rio Carnival to the 2016 Summer Olympics.

The residents of Rio de Janeiro are very proud of their city and its distinct way of life. Rio de Janeiro is a popular tourist destination for people from all walks of life, thanks to its colorful culture and beautiful beaches.

Religion

Rio de Janeiro has a rich religious and spiritual tradition. With an estimated 88.4% of the population identifying as Catholic, Catholicism is the most popular religion in Rio.

The bulk of the population is Roman Catholic, although other Christian faiths such as Adventists, Pentecostals, and Baptists are also present. Judaism, Islam, Buddhism, and Spiritism are also minority faiths.

In Rio de Janeiro, Catholicism has a long and significant history. Rio hosted the first Catholic service in 1567, and the city has been a prominent center of Catholic life ever since.

The Metropolitan Cathedral of St. Sebastian, the
Lady of the Candelaria, and the Church of St. Fra
Rio's most notable religious landmarks. All of the
the city center and are accessible to the public.

Rio has a significant Catholic influence, with several churches and
religious groups working in the city. The Catholic University of Rio
de Janeiro is the city's major institution, and there are many Catholic
hospitals and organizations.

**The Church also has a political role, with the Archbishop
of Rio de Janeiro being a major figure in the city.**

Chapter 2

DISCOVER RIO DE JANEIRO

Rio de Janeiro is noted for its stunning vistas of the Atlantic Ocean and surrounding mountains, as well as its famous sites, such as the Christ the Redeemer statue and Sugar loaf Peak.

The city has some of the greatest beaches in the world, including Copacabana and Ipanema, as well as world-class nightlife, shopping, and cuisine. Rio has it all, whether you're seeking for a romantic getaway or an exciting adventure.

Rio de Janeiro also has a thriving art and cultural scene, with galleries and museums highlighting the city's distinct history and culture. From the bohemian ambience of Lapa to the ancient areas of Santa Teresa and Botafogo, there's plenty to pique your interest.

Of course, no trip to Rio is complete without experiencing the city's legendary Carnival, which is one of the world's biggest and most colorful festivities.

Rio de Janeiro is the ideal spot for a romantic holiday, an action-packed adventure, or just a place to rest and take in the scenery. Rio offers something for everyone, with its gorgeous surroundings, rich culture, and thrilling nightlife.

Therefore, be ready to explore and experience Rio de Janeiro's treasures!

Weather and Climate

Rio de Janeiro is a seaside city in Brazil's southern region. It is the state capital of Rio de Janeiro and Brazil's second most populated city. Rio de Janeiro has a tropical climate due to its position on the Atlantic Ocean and the presence of mountains.

Rio de Janeiro's climate is typically warm and humid all year, with temperatures ranging from roughly 18 degrees Celsius in winter to around 26 degrees Celsius in summer.

The city has two different seasons: the rainy season and the dry season. The rainy season lasts from November to March and is marked by cloudy sky and heavy rain. The dry season, which lasts from April to October, is distinguished by bright sky, low humidity, and mild breezes.

Extreme weather phenomena such as storms, floods, and droughts are also common in Rio de Janeiro. Hurricanes are regular in the region, with the most recent one, Hurricane Catarina, striking in 2004.

Flooding is also frequent, with the most recent occurrence happening in 2011. Droughts, on the other hand, are uncommon, with the most recent happening in 2018.

Rio de Janeiro receives around 1,700 millimeters of rain each year, with the majority of it falling during the rainy season. The average yearly temperature is roughly 25 degrees Celsius, with December and January being the warmest months and June and July being the coolest.

Rio de Janeiro has a warm and humid climate, with temperatures ranging from 18 degrees Celsius in winter to roughly 26 degrees Celsius in summer. Hurricanes, floods, and droughts are all possible in the city, although they are uncommon. The yearly rainfall averages roughly 1,700 millimeters, with the most of it occurring during the rainy season.

Population

Rio de Janeiro is Brazil's second biggest city and one of the most populated in South America. It is situated in the country's southern part, and its metropolitan area has a population of more than 12 million people.

The city is well-known for its beautiful beaches, lively culture, and spectacular scenery. It has grown into a significant tourist attraction, attracting millions of people each year from all over the globe.

Rio de Janeiro's population is expected to be 6.5 million people, with an annual population growth rate of 1.4%. Around 70% of the population is mixed race, with 24% of African heritage. With a median age of 30.3 years, the population is fairly youthful. Around 95% of the population is literate.

Rio de Janeiro's economy is mostly centered on tourism, although the city is also a significant port and a financial and industrial powerhouse. The GDP of the city is expected to be more than $100 billion.

The predominant languages spoken in Rio de Janeiro are Portuguese and English, with some people also speaking Spanish and French. The city offers a thriving nightlife as well as a diverse selection of cultural events.

It also hosts a number of major events, including the world's biggest street celebration, Carnival, and the Rio de Janeiro International Film Festival.

Rio de Janeiro's population has been gradually expanding over the last several decades and is likely to continue to rise in the future years. The city has a diversified and dynamic culture, and it is a key financial, industrial, and tourist hub

Delicious & Nutritious Meal

•Feijoada: This hearty stew of black beans and pork is considered Brazil's national cuisine.

•Churrasco: Grilled meats such as beef, hog, chicken, and sausages that are served with a variety of sides.

•Moqueca: A coconut milk and spice-cooked fish dish.

•Acarajé: Deep-fried black-eyed pea fritters with vatapá on top (a blend of shrimp, coconut milk, peanuts, and palm oil).

•Brigadeiro: A well-known Brazilian chocolate truffle.

•Coxinha is a deep-fried chicken croquette.

•Po de Queijo: Cheese bread.

•Quibebe: A dish of squash and maize.

•Aça: A frozen smoothie prepared with aça berries and other fruits combined together.

•Caipirinha: Brazil's national drink, prepared of cachaça, sugar, and lime.

Currency

The Brazilian Real is the currency of Rio de Janeiro, Brazil (BRL). The Brazilian Real, which has been in circulation since 1994, is the native currency of Rio de Janeiro. The Brazilian Real is denominated in centavos. "R$" is the symbol for the Real.

The Real is the most extensively used currency in Brazil and is issued by the Central Bank of Brazil. Other nations that utilize it include Argentina, Uruguay, and Paraguay.

The Brazilian Real's exchange rate is set by the foreign exchange market. The value of the Real is influenced by the economy, inflation rate, and political stability of the nation

It is essential to convert your cash for the Brazilian Real before leaving your native nation while visiting Rio de Janeiro. This will allow you to avoid any extra conversion costs and make the most of your money

While visiting Rio de Janeiro, it is also important to be mindful of the shifting currency rate. The exchange rate may fluctuate fast, therefore it is important to be aware of the current rate before exchanging money.

The majority of Rio de Janeiro's main banks provide currency exchange services. You may also exchange currencies at a money exchange station at the airport or in tourist regions. Save all of your receipts after exchanging money, since they may be turned back into the original currency at the conclusion of your stay.

Credit cards are usually accepted in Rio de Janeiro; however, verify with your bank before traveling to guarantee that your card will be accepted. It is also critical to tell your bank that you will be visiting Rio de Janeiro so that your card is not stopped for suspicious behavior.

It is also possible to withdraw money from ATM in Rio de Janeiro; however, you should check to see whether there are any costs before doing so.

While visiting Rio de Janeiro, it is essential to understand the currency and conversion rates so that you can make the most of your money.

ATM & Locations

ATM may be located in a number of venues in Rio de Janeiro, including banks, post offices, supermarkets, airports, and even on the street.

1. **Bank do Brasil: Many branches**

2. **Banco Santander: Many branches**

3. Banco Ita: Many sites

4. Bradesco: Many places

5. Caixa Econômica Federal: Many sites

6. HSBC: Numerous branches

**7. Po de Açcar Supermarket:
   Numerous Locations**

8. Extra Supermarket: Several Locations

9. Terminal 1 at Rio de Janeiro-Galeo International Airport

10. Terminal 1 at Santos Dumont Airport

Official language

Rio de Janeiro is the capital of Brazil and one of the world's most populated cities. It is well-known for its stunning beaches, lively nightlife, and different cultures.

Rio de Janeiro's official language is Brazilian Portuguese, which is also the most frequently spoken language in the nation.

Brazilian Portuguese derives from the Portuguese language, which was introduced to the country by Portuguese colonists in the 16th century. It has been strongly impacted by other languages spoken in the area, particularly Native American and African languages, since its introduction.

As a consequence, Brazilian Portuguese has a distinct taste and character that can be detected in the region's music and literature.

The language is spoken by practically everyone in Rio de Janeiro, making it the city's main language. It is also spoken in other regions of the nation, albeit there are minor regional differences.

The language is used in a variety of areas, including as business, education, and the media. It's also common in regular interactions and the media. Rio de Janeiro is home to several distinct dialects of Brazilian Portuguese, thus it is essential to understand the differences while interacting.

Since Portuguese is the language of government and commerce in Brazil, it is essential for visitors and residents of Rio de Janeiro to learn the language. It is also beneficial to acquire a few essential words and idioms in order to engage with city dwellers.

Public Holidays

Rio de Janeiro is recognized for its colorful culture, culture, and festivals, so it's no surprise that it has several public holidays throughout the year. There is something for everyone to celebrate, from Carnival to Christmas. Below is a list of some of Rio de Janeiro's most prominent public holidays.

1. New Year's Day (January 1): This is the formal start of the new year, and it is celebrated across the city with parades and fireworks.

2. Carnival (February/March): One of Rio de Janeiro's most renowned festivities, it takes place before Lent. Around the city, there are parades, street celebrations, and samba contests.

3. Tiradentes Day (April 21): This festival remembers Tiradentes' sacrifice in the fight for Brazilian independence from Portugal.

4. Labor Day (May 1): This is a day set aside to honor and celebrate workers' rights.

5. Corpus Christi (June): This is a Catholic celebration that commemorates Jesus Christ's body and blood.

6. Independence Day (September 7): This is a national holiday commemorating Brazil's independence from Portugal in 1822.

7. All Souls' Day (November 2): A day to commemorate and respect the deceased.

8. Christmas (December 25): This festive celebration commemorates the birth of Jesus Christ.

9. New Year's Eve (December 31): This is the final day of the year, and it is celebrated across the city with fireworks and festivities.

These are only a few of Rio de Janeiro's public holidays. There are also other state and municipal holidays to consider when organizing a vacation.

Dos & Don't

Do's:

1. **Dress modestly** - Rio de Janeiro is renowned for its beaches and hot weather, so dress accordingly for the culture and weather. Wearing exposing apparel, such as short shorts, tank tops, and tube tops, is discouraged.

2. **Make an attempt to learn some Portuguese** - While many people in Rio de Janeiro speak English, it is always welcomed when

tourists make an effort to learn some Portuguese in order to converse with locals.

3. **Carry tiny cash** - Little banknotes are difficult to come by in Rio de Janeiro, so have some on hand for modest purchases.

4. **Use public transit** - The public transportation system in Rio de Janeiro is safe and efficient, so using the bus or metro is a fantastic way to travel about the city.

5. **Go to the beaches** - Rio de Janeiro is famed for its beautiful beaches, so spend some time relaxing on the sand and admiring the scenery.

6. **Be alert of your surroundings** - Rio de Janeiro is a vast metropolis with certain sections being more hazardous than others. Keep an eye on your surroundings and don't go off by yourself.

Donts:

1. **Do not carry huge sums of cash** - Carrying large sums of cash is never a smart idea and might make you a target for criminals.

2. **Keep your valuables** near and don't leave them unattended - Keep your valuables close and don't leave them unattended.

3. **Do not photograph military or government buildings -** Photographing military or government structures is prohibited and may result in prosecution.

4. **Don't take beverages from strangers** - It's always a good idea to be careful and refuse drinks from strangers.

5. **Don't show off your money or jewelry** - Showing off your money or jewelry might make you a target for criminals.

6. **Avoid wearing costly clothes or jewelry** - Expensive clothing and jewelry might make you a target for criminals, so avoid wearing them.

Sacred Architecture

Rio de Janeiro's sacred architecture has a long and rich history. It reflects the history, culture, and beliefs of the city. Rio de Janeiro was established in 1565 by the Portuguese and swiftly grew to become one of the major cities in the Americas.

The city's ecclesiastical architecture expanded with it. Around the city, churches, chapels, convents, and monasteries were constructed, typically with elegant and complex architecture.

The Metropolitan Cathedral of Saint Sebastian, completed in the late 1800s, is Rio de Janeiro's most prominent holy building. The cathedral is the biggest church in the Americas and often regarded as one of the most beautiful in the world.

It is a Neo-Gothic edifice that is ornately embellished with sculptures, stained glass, and elaborate decorations. The cathedral also holds numerous notable religious artworks, like as Bernardo Pinto de Almeida's picture of Saint Sebastian.

The Church of Our Lady of the Candelaria is another significant piece of holy architecture in Rio de Janeiro. This Baroque-style church, erected in 1688, is situated in the city center.

The gold-plated altar, marble sculptures, and exquisite ceiling paintings are among the church's most notable embellishments.

Many famous religious artworks, including paintings of Saint Francis of Assisi and the Virgin Mary, may also be seen at the Church of Our Lady of the Candelaria.

Another significant example of holy architecture in Rio de Janeiro is the Monastery of Saint Benedict. The monastery was founded in 1612 and is one of the city's oldest ecclesiastical structures.

It is a stunning example of Baroque architecture, featuring statues, arches, and other decorative embellishments on the façade.

A crucifix and a wooden figure of Saint Benedict are among the sacred treasures housed at the monastery.

Rio de Janeiro's Sacred Art Museum is also an essential aspect of the city's religious architecture. The museum includes a rich collection of religious art dating from the sixteenth to the nineteenth century. Famous painters such as Bernardo Pinto de Almeida and Aleijadinho have works on display at the museum.

Rio de Janeiro's sacred architecture reflects the city's history, culture, and beliefs. These structures, ranging from the grandiose Metropolitan Cathedral of Saint Sebastian to the Monastery of Saint Benedict, are significant components of the city's religious legacy.

The Rio de Janeiro Sacred Art Museum also offers a unique look into the city's religious history and culture.

Cultural standards and restrictions

Rio de Janeiro is a bustling and interesting city with a diverse spectrum of cultures and people. As a first-time tourist to the city, it is essential to understand the cultural norms and regulations in place to guarantee a safe and pleasurable stay.

It is vital to dress cautiously while entering any public venue in Rio de Janeiro. This includes avoiding too exposing clothing, which is considered rude in most circumstances.

It's also worth noting that public shows of love, such as kissing and holding hands, are often frowned upon and should be avoided.

It is also crucial to understand the etiquette of greetings in Rio de Janeiro. In general, greeting someone with a handshake and a nice grin is considered courteous. Eye contact is also essential since it is seen as a show of respect.

It is crucial to dress correctly and act politely while visiting religious places in Rio de Janeiro. Shorts, tank tops, and flip-flops should be avoided, and visitors should be careful of their behavior while near a sacred structure.

In terms of language, Portuguese is the official language of Brazil, therefore tourists visiting Rio de Janeiro should take the time to acquire a few fundamental words.

This will come in handy in a variety of circumstances, from ordering meals at a restaurant to asking for directions.

Lastly, it is important to understand the local legislation of Rio de Janeiro. This includes avoiding behaviors like public drinking and smoking in non-designated smoking places, which may result in substantial penalties.

Visitors will have a safe and happy trip if they follow the cultural norms and regulations of Rio de Janeiro.

Local laws

The Brazilian Constitution serves as the basic source of legislation in Rio de Janeiro and across the nation. It defines people' basic rights and ensures their freedom. Moreover, the Constitution establishes the organization of the government and the laws for elections.

Rio de Janeiro has its own set of rules that govern the city and its residents. These laws are classified into three categories: civil, criminal, and administrative.

Civil law governs interpersonal interactions such as contracts, property ownership, and torts. Family law, which controls marriage, divorce, and adoption, is also included.

Criminal law is intended to safeguard the public by punishing criminals. It also specifies which behaviors are unlawful and what penalties are acceptable for individuals who violate the law.

Administrative law is concerned with government acts and company regulation. It establishes the norms and processes to be followed when interacting with government entities, such as when asking for permissions or licenses.

Rio de Janeiro is is subject to a variety of unique laws. They include legislation governing tourism, environmental protection, public safety, and cultural heritage preservation.

In addition to municipal laws, the Brazilian Federal Government has laws that apply across the nation. Federal organizations such as the Federal Police and the Ministry of Justice execute these laws.

Rio de Janeiro has signed a number of international treaties and accords. The Brazilian government enforces these treaties and accords, which are obligatory on all people.

Rio de Janeiro's municipal laws are intended to enhance the safety and welfare of its residents while also protecting their rights.

The laws are intended to guarantee that all residents are treated equally and have access to justice.

Chapter 3

ITINERARY BASIC CLUES FOR ENTRY

1. **Passport:** All visitors to Rio de Janeiro are required to have a valid passport.

2. **Visa**: Depending on your country, you may need a visa to visit Rio de Janeiro.

3. **Health requirements**: Some nations may require passengers to provide evidence of vaccination against certain illnesses before entering.

4. **Flight details**: Before your admission is permitted, you must furnish the Brazilian government with your travel information, including dates, times, and flight numbers.

5. **Financial information:** You will also be required to provide evidence of financial resources to sustain your stay in Rio de Janeiro. A credit card, bank statement, or other financial document might be included.

Visa Requirements

The nation of origin will determine the visa requirements for entry into Rio de Janeiro. Several nations, including the United States, Australia, Canada, and the United Kingdom, do not need a visa to visit Rio de Janeiro and will be issued a 90-day tourist visa upon arrival. This visa is extendable for another 90 days.

Some countries, like China, India, and several South American nations, need a visa to enter. Visas must be acquired ahead of time from a Brazilian embassy or consulate. These nations' visa requirements may include evidence of travel insurance, proof of a return flight, and a valid passport.

Also, all visitors entering Brazil must provide a valid yellow fever certificate. This certificate is valid for ten years and must be acquired at least ten days before entering Brazil.

Who is required to get visa to Rio de Janeiro

Visitors to Rio de Janeiro must get a visa before arriving. Apart for inhabitants of specific countries, all foreign nationals entering Brazil must have a valid visa. Nationals of Argentina, Bolivia, Chile, Colombia, Ecuador, Paraguay, Peru, Uruguay, and Venezuela are excluded from the visa requirement if they are visiting Brazil for tourism, business, or transit and their stay does not exceed 90 days.

Citizens of nations not excluded from the visa requirement must apply for a visa before visiting Brazil. Depending on the purpose of the visit, there are various different kinds of visas available.

The tourist visa is the most prevalent form of visa. Tourist visas are valid for 90 days and may be renewed for another 90 days. Business visas, which are normally valid for up to 180 days, are also available for persons traveling for work reasons.

To apply for a visa, candidates must complete an online application form and submit the necessary papers. A valid passport, a completed visa application form, two passport-size pictures, evidence of financial means, proof of travel plans, and a valid immunization certificate are often needed for a visa application.

It is crucial to know that the visa application procedure might take up to 30 days, so apply for the visa well ahead of your anticipated trip date.

After the visa has been accepted, the applicant must pick it up at the Brazilian Consulate or Embassy in his or her home country. Upon arrival in Brazil, the visa must be shown to immigration officers.

If you do not have a valid visa when you enter Brazil, you may face a fine, expulsion, or both. It's also worth noting that visas must be utilized within 90 days after being issued. After the visa expires, the holder must apply for a new one.

Short term visa Application

Rio de Janeiro is one of the most popular tourist destinations in the world, famed for its lively culture, beautiful beaches, and panoramic city vistas. It should be noted that entering Brazil needs a visa.

A short-term visa is necessary for people intending a short-term stay in Rio de Janeiro. A short-term visa is valid for up to 90 days and may be renewed for up to 180 days in a year.

The following papers must be submitted to the Brazilian Embassy in order to apply for a short-term visa to Rio de Janeiro:

• A valid passport valid for at least six months beyond the date of entrance into Brazil

• A visa application form that has been completed

• A passport-sized picture

• Evidence of enough cash to support the length of your stay in Brazil

• A duplicate of a valid return or onward travel ticket

• A copy of a valid hotel reservation or evidence of lodging in Brazil

• Evidence of work or education in the home country

• Evidence of medical insurance

• Any additional documents that is relevant

Applicants must additionally pay a visa fee and, in certain cases, appear in person at the Brazilian Consulate. It should be noted that the visa application procedure might take several weeks, so candidates should apply well ahead of their desired trip dates.

Document needed to apply for visa for Rio de Janeiro

An applicant must provide the following papers in order to apply for a visa to Rio de Janeiro:

• *A completed visa application form*

• *A valid passport*

• *Two passport-sized pictures*
• *A letter of invitation from a Brazilian host (if applicable)*

• *Any other documentation requested by the Brazilian embassy or consulate*

Chapter 4

GETTING AROUND

Rio de Janeiro, Brazil's former capital, is one of the world's most dynamic cities. Visitors visit the city's beaches, samba clubs, and other attractions in droves.

But, in order to really appreciate what Rio de Janeiro has to offer, visitors must be how to navigate the city. Fortunately, the city provides a range of transit alternatives, including buses, taxis, and ferries.

Buses are the most common kind of public transportation for getting about the city. In Rio de Janeiro, buses are classified into two types: regular buses and express buses. Regular buses are the most affordable and readily accessible, however they might be sluggish owing to traffic.

Express buses are more costly than regular buses, but they are quicker and more efficient. The city also features a fast bus transportation system, known as BRT, which is an excellent alternative for individuals wishing to travel swiftly and effectively.

Taxis, in addition to buses, are a common mode of transportation in Rio de Janeiro. Taxis are reasonably priced, and they may be hailed on the street or reserved in advance. It is important to highlight that it is advisable to take only legal taxis, since unregistered taxis may be harmful.

Air Transportation

Rio de Janeiro is a bustling city with a variety of transportation alternatives for tourists. For first-time tourists, air travel is the most convenient and effective method to get to and from Rio de Janeiro.

Rio de Janeiro is served by many airports, including Rio de Janeiro-Galeo International Airport (GIG) and Santos Dumont Airport (SDU). Rio de Janeiro-Galeo International Airport (GIG) is the city's major airport, situated about 20 kilometers from the city center.

It is Brazil's biggest airport and one of the busiest in South America. The airport offers direct international flights to over 100 destinations worldwide, as well as regional and local flights.

Santos Dumont Airport (SDU) is situated in downtown Rio de Janeiro and is the city's second airport. It is a smaller airport with fewer international connections, but it is a more convenient choice for those who wish to stay near to the city center.

There are various ways to travel to your destination after you arrive at the airport. At the airport, you may take a cab to your hotel or destination. Taxis are accessible at both airports, and reservations may be made online or at the taxi stand. The fee will be determined by the distance and may vary between 30 and 50 BRL (Brazilian Reais).

You may also take a bus from the airport to your destination. Buses are accessible at both airports and travel around the city on a regular basis. The fare is around 10 BRL per person.

You may also take the Metro to your location from the airport. For passengers who need to get there fast, the Metro is a practical and cost-effective solution. The fare is around 6 BRL per person.

Ultimately, you have the option of taking a shuttle or a private transport. Both airports include shuttles and private transfers that will transport you straight to your destination.

The cost of shuttles and private transportation may vary depending on distance, but will typically range between 50 and 100 BRL.

Whichever mode of transportation you pick, remember to account for any extra expenses, such as tolls or tips. Also, certain transit alternatives may be unavailable at specific times of day or on certain days of the week, so it is important to plan ahead and schedule transportation in advance.

Land transportation

Rio de Janeiro, Brazil's capital, is a bustling metropolis rich in culture and history. Rio de Janeiro is a popular tourist destination due to its beautiful beaches and active nightlife.

Before visiting Rio, it is essential to understand how to move about. Rio de Janeiro is served by several modes of ground transportation, including buses, taxis, and automobile rentals.

In Rio de Janeiro, buses are the most common mode of public transit. The city's public bus system is run by the municipal government and is reasonably priced.

Local buses run along predetermined routes across the city and cost around R$3.50 per ride. Monthly and annual bus tickets are offered for travelers staying for an extended length of time.

Taxis are another common mode of transportation in Rio. Taxis are commonly accessible around the city and may be located at authorized taxi stations.

Taxis may also be hired by the hour or day. Taxis vary in price, but as a general rule, rates start about R$15 and escalate based on distance traveled.

In Rio de Janeiro, you may also hire a car. There are various automobile rental firms situated across the city, and costs vary based on the kind of vehicle and length of hire. It should be noted that drivers in Brazil must have an international driver's license.

Generally, ground transportation in Rio de Janeiro is reasonably priced. Bus prices begin about R$3.50, while taxi costs begin around R$15. Vehicle rental fees vary depending on the kind of vehicle and the length of the rental term, but they normally begin at R$70/day.

A monthly or annual bus ticket may be the most cost-effective alternative for travellers staying in Rio de Janeiro for an extended length of time.

Train Transportation

Train transit in Rio de Janeiro is a popular and convenient mode of transportation. Many railroad lines operate across the city, linking various regions of the city and making travel simpler. Rio de Janeiro has two major railway lines: the SuperVia and the MetroRio.

The SuperVia rail line, which travels across the city, is the most popular. It runs from 5:00 a.m. to midnight and has a variety of routes, making it simple to reach to practically any location in the city.

The train is divided into two classes: express and regional. Express provides better comfort and speedier travel times, whilst Regional is less expensive. Regional tickets cost R$2.30 (US$0.45), while Express tickets cost R$4.30 (US$0.84).

The MetroRio is Rio de Janeiro's second rail line. It is a smaller, more contemporary system that runs from 5:30 a.m. until 12:00 a.m. The MetroRio is divided into two classes: Metro and SuperVia. Metro provides better comfort and quicker travel times, although SuperVia is less expensive. SuperVia costs R$2.30 (US$0.45), while Metro costs R$4.30 (US$0.84).

Overall, rail travel in Rio de Janeiro is a convenient and cost-effective alternative. The two major lines provide varying levels of service and rates, allowing tourists to choose the best choice for their requirements. Moreover, the rail lines run late into the night, making it simple to navigate about the city.

Sea Transportation

In Rio de Janeiro, Brazil, sea transportation is an essential mode of transportation. It is a large port, through which numerous products imported and exported to and from Brazil travel.

The Port of Rio de Janeiro, situated in the city's industrial zone, is one of South America's major ports, handling more than 30 million tons of cargo yearly. Rio de Janeiro, in addition to being a significant port, is also an important cruising and yachting centre.

Ferries are the most prevalent mode of maritime transportation in Rio de Janeiro. Ferries are a quick and inexpensive method to move about the city. Ferries run from downtown Rio to Copacabana, Ipanema, and Leblon beaches, as well as the islands of Ilha Grande and Angra dos Reis. A one-way ferry ticket costs around 5-10 Real (the Brazilian currency).

In Rio de Janeiro, cruise ships are also an entertaining mode of transportation. Cruise ships travel from Rio de Janeiro and visit ports along Brazil's coast, including Ilha Grande, Angra dos Reis, and Salvador. Prices for a 4-5 day trip might vary from $200 and $500 USD per person, depending on the itinerary.

Apart from ferries and cruise ships, Rio de Janeiro features a variety of private yachts for rent. Chartering a yacht for a day excursion normally costs between $500 and $1,000 USD, depending on the size of the boat and the length of the voyage.

Generally, Rio de Janeiro has a wide range of maritime transportation choices. Costs vary based on the mode of transportation and the length of the journey. When arranging a vacation, it is important to explore the best choice for your budget and requirements.

Rental services

For tourists visiting Rio de Janeiro, a number of transportation rental options are available. Prices might vary depending on the sort of rental service you want.

Taxis are a popular mode of transportation in Rio de Janeiro, and the cost of a taxi journey is determined by distance and time of day. In the city center, a cab journey normally costs between R$10.00 and R$15.00 (about US$2.50 to US$3.75).

Car Rental: Avis, Hertz, Europcar, and Localiza are among the various automobile rental firms in Rio de Janeiro. The cost of hiring a vehicle is determined by the automobile's size and the duration of the rental period. Pricing per day may vary between R$100.00 and R$200.00 (about US$25.00 to US$50.00).

Bus: Public buses are a common mode of transportation in Rio de Janeiro, and they may be an inexpensive way to get about. A single bus ticket costs R$3.00 (around $0.75 USD).

Uber: Uber is accessible in Rio de Janeiro and is a quick and simple method to travel about. The cost of an Uber trip in the city center is between R$15.00 and R$20.00 (about US$3.75 to US$5.00) based on the kind of vehicle and the distance traveled.

Bicycle: In Rio de Janeiro, bicycle rental firms such as BikRio and Mobike provide bicycle rental services. The hourly rate ranges from R$10.00 to R$20.00 (about US$2.50 to US$5.00).

Chapter 5

RIO DE JANEIRO AREA BY AREA

Rio de Janeiro is a well-known city in Brazil's southern area. It is one of the world's most visited cities and home to some of the country's most recognizable sites.

Rio de Janeiro is a city that will steal your breath away, from the magnificent beaches of Copacabana and Ipanema to the amazing vistas of the Christ the Redeemer monument atop Corcovado mountain.

Rio de Janeiro is separated into various zones. The city center, or Centro, is the city's oldest neighborhood and home to many of the city's most prominent landmarks.

The iconic Praca XV de Novembro, the Museum of Art of Rio de Janeiro, and the Theatro Municipal are all located here. Several of the city's financial and commercial areas are also located in Centro.

The city's most frequented region is the South Zone. It is the location of the world-famous Copacabana and Ipanema beaches, as well as some of the city's most opulent hotels, restaurants, and nightlife. Sugarloaf Mountain, which gives excellent views of the city, is also located in this region.

The West Zone is a residential district on the other side of the harbor from Centro. Several of the city's most popular parks may be found here, including Tijuca National Park, the world's biggest urban forest. Several of the city's most wealthy neighborhoods, including Barra da Tijuca, Recreio dos Bandeirantes, and Jacarepagua, are also located in this region.

The North Zone is the city's most populated district and is home to several of the city's favelas. Several of the city's cultural attractions, like as the Maracana Stadium and the Sambadrome, are located in this district, which is noted for its colorful culture.

The East Zone is the city's least frequented neighborhood. Some of the city's most stunning vistas may be seen here, including amazing views of the Christ the Redeemer monument atop Corcovado mountain.

Several of the city's oldest neighborhoods, such as Santa Teresa and Lapa, are also located in this region.

Whichever part of Rio de Janeiro you visit, you will undoubtedly discover something that will take your breath away. Rio de Janeiro is a city that will leave you with amazing experiences, from the magnificent beaches of Copacabana and Ipanema to the vivid culture of the favelas and the spectacular views of the Christ the Redeemer monument.

Chapter 6

PLANNING YOUR TRIP

Travel planning can be an exciting and rewarding activity. It enables you to go to new locations, meet new people, and learn about diverse cultures. It may, however, be stressful and upsetting.

This travel guide will assist you in making the most of your vacation and making it a memorable experience.

Arranging a vacation enables you to prepare your budget as well. You may choose how much money you want to spend on lodging, meals, and activities. This will assist you in budgeting for any unforeseen expenditures that may arise during your vacation.

Another advantage of planning a vacation is that it allows you to construct an itinerary. This will assist you in keeping track of your activities and ensuring that you do not miss anything. You can also ensure that you are getting the finest offers and discount

These are just a few of the many advantages of arranging a vacation. You can ensure the success of your vacation with a little study and planning.

Getting to Rio de Janeiro

For a first-time tourist, getting to Rio de Janeiro is reasonably simple, with a variety of transportation alternatives.

By Air

Rio de Janeiro is served by two international airports: Galeo International Airport (GIG) and Santos Dumont Airport (SDU) (SDU). Galeo International Airport is the bigger and more popular of the two, serving as the primary international gateway.

All of the main airlines fly to and from the airport, and there are many connections from places all over the globe. The airport is roughly 20 kilometers north of Rio de Janeiro's downtown area and is readily accessible by taxi, bus, or vehicle.

By Sea

There are other cruise ships that go to and from Rio de Janeiro. Numerous cruise companies offer itineraries that include stops in destinations other than Rio de Janeiro. It is critical to double-check the schedule ahead of time to ensure that the cruise includes a stop in Rio de Janeiro.

By Bus

Rio de Janeiro is well linked by bus to other cities in Brazil. There are many bus companies that provide daily service to the city. Tickets must be purchased in advance since buses fill up rapidly.

Taking the Train

Rio de Janeiro is also accessible by rail from other Brazilian cities. The trains are pleasant and reasonably priced. The travel time varies based on the route used.

By Car

For first-time tourists, driving to Rio de Janeiro is not suggested. The roads in Brazil may be treacherous, therefore you should travel with an experienced driver.

When you arrive in Rio de Janeiro, there are several ways to navigate about the city. The city offers a public bus system, as well as taxis and Uber. There are also several automobile rental agencies in the city.

How to save up for your trip

1. **Create a budget**: When you begin saving, make sure you have an exact estimate of how much money you'll need to pay all of your Rio de Janeiro costs. Lodging, transportation, food, entertainment, and any other incidentals should be included.

2. **Establish a goal**: After you've established a budget, choose how much you want to save. This should be practical and doable given the constraints of your trip's timetable.

3. **Reduce your expenditure**: Seek for methods to reduce your spending. This may be as easy as taking your lunch to work or reducing needless purchases.

4. **Seek for travel offers**: When booking flights, hotels, and other travel services, look for discounts and specials. Look for travel rewards credit cards that provide discounts or reward points.

5. **Use a savings account**: Create a separate savings account for your vacation. This will keep you on track and prevent you from dipping into your money for other purposes.

6. **Save any additional money**: Any excess income, such as bonuses or tax returns, should go immediately into your vacation savings account.

Traveling Alone

Rio de Janeiro is one of the world's most dynamic cities, and many people want to visit there. The prospect of traveling alone adds to some people's excitement about visiting Rio de Janeiro. Going alone to Rio de Janeiro is an exciting and unique experience, but it is vital to prepare ahead of time and be aware of the possible hazards.

While going alone to Rio de Janeiro, it is essential to do comprehensive study ahead of time. You should get acquainted with the city, its neighborhoods, and its culture. It is also critical to grasp local laws and traditions, as well as how to keep safe in the city. Learning a few basic Portuguese words can also help you converse with locals.

While traveling alone to Rio de Janeiro, it is recommended to stay in a secure hotel or hostel. Consider sleeping in a shared hostel or an Airbnb if you're seeking for a more affordable choice. Before making a reservation, read the reviews and verify the area's safety.

It is also essential to organize your transportation while in Rio de Janeiro. Public transportation is the most cost-effective choice, but it is vital to be mindful of the possible threats, such as pick pocketing. If you are uneasy about using public transit, you may also use taxis or ride-sharing services like Uber.

Another precaution to take while traveling alone to Rio de Janeiro is to keep your belongings secure. Keep your passport, money, and other critical papers in a safe, secure location at all times. It is also important to be aware of your surroundings and to believe your intuition. If you ever feel uncomfortable, go to a safe area right away.

Traveling alone to Rio de Janeiro may be an exciting and one-of-a-kind experience. It is important to prepare ahead of time and be aware of the hazards connected with a solo journey. With proper planning, you can ensure that your vacation is safe, fun, and memorable.

Traveling With children

Traveling to Rio de Janeiro with children can be an exciting and gratifying experience for everyone concerned. Rio de Janeiro's colorful and distinct culture, along with the city's breathtaking surroundings and lovely beaches, make it an ideal family trip. You can ensure that your family vacation to Rio de Janeiro runs smoothly and is as pleasurable as possible by organizing ahead of time.

While planning your vacation to Rio de Janeiro, keep your children's ages in mind, as well as the activities they will like. Rio de Janeiro offers a diverse choice of activities, sights, and experiences to offer families, making it an excellent vacation for people of all ages.

The beaches of Copacabana and Ipanema, the Christ the Redeemer monument, Sugarloaf Mountain, and the Sambodrome are among the most prominent attractions in Rio de Janeiro. Before you go, be sure to verify the age limitations of any attractions you want to visit.

While going to Rio de Janeiro, you should also consider your children's safety. Rio de Janeiro, like any major city, has its share of crime, so it's necessary to remain alert of your surroundings and practice basic safety measures.

Avoid going alone at night and use extreme care in congested locations. It is also advisable to store your valuables out of sight and in a safe place.

Bring a choice of clothes ideal for both warm and chilly weather while packing for your vacation to Rio de Janeiro. Rio de Janeiro has a tropical climate, so bring light, breathable clothes. Under the blazing Brazilian heat, sunscreen and hats are also essential. If you are traveling with little children, prepare lots of food, diapers, and other things to keep them comfortable.

Lastly, before traveling to Rio de Janeiro, learn about the local traditions and culture. The Brazilian people are kind and inviting, and visitors should respect their culture and traditions. Learn the local language and remember to be respectful to religious places and other cultural monuments.

Traveling to Rio de Janeiro with children may be a memorable experience for the whole family. With some careful preparation and regard for your children's needs, you can guarantee that the trip is both safe and fun for everyone.

Reasons you should visit

Rio de Janeiro is a lively, busy metropolis with something for everyone. Rio de Janeiro offers it everything, whether you want a quiet beach holiday, an active nightlife, or a cultural experience. These are eight reasons to visit Rio de Janeiro.

1. Rio de Janeiro is well-known for its **beautiful beaches.** There's something for everyone, from the most popular locations, Copacabana and Ipanema, to the laid-back Barra da Tijuca and the serene Prainha.

2. **Amazing Nightlife:** Rio de Janeiro is a city that never sleeps, and its nightlife is world-renowned. You'll find something to your liking, from samba clubs to rooftop pubs.

3. **Cultural Heritage:** Rio de Janeiro has a rich cultural legacy, which is seen in its architecture, museums, and festivals. Enjoy a walking tour of the ancient town, visit museums and galleries, or watch a samba parade.

4. **Delectable Food**: Rio de Janeiro is a gastronomic paradise. There's something for everyone's taste buds, from colorful street cuisine to exquisite dining.

5. **Fantastic Shopping:** Rio de Janeiro offers everything for everyone, from traditional markets to sophisticated malls. Purchase clothing, souvenirs, and everything in between.

6. **Tropical Climate**: Rio de Janeiro has a tropical climate that is ideal for sunbathing and other outdoor activities.

7. **Adventure Activities:** Rio de Janeiro is ideal for daring sports such as bungee jumping, cliff leaping, and paragliding.

8. **Pleasant People**: The inhabitants of Rio de Janeiro are pleasant and inviting. You're bound to meet some new people.

Thus, if you're seeking for a one-of-a-kind vacation destination, try Rio de Janeiro. You're guaranteed to have a terrific trip with its magnificent beaches, bustling nightlife, rich culture, amazing cuisine, great shopping, fabulous weather, adventurous activities, and nice people.

Best time to visit

Rio de Janeiro is one of the world's most popular tourist attractions. It is no wonder that it is a popular tourist destination, with its beautiful beaches, historic sites, and lively culture.

If you want to go on a beach vacation, the ideal time to visit Rio de Janeiro is between December and March. The beaches are at their finest during the hottest and driest months of the year. This is, however, the busiest and most costly time to visit.

The ideal time to visit Rio de Janeiro if you want to save money is between April and November. This is normally the off-season, therefore it is less expensive to come at this time. You will also notice that there are less people and that the rates of lodging and activities are reduced.

It should also be mentioned that during the summer months, Rio de Janeiro may be rather hot and humid. If you're planning a vacation around this period, be prepared for intense heat and excessive humidity.

Whenever time of year you come, Rio de Janeiro will give you with a memorable experience. It is one of the most popular tourist destinations in the world, thanks to its beautiful beaches, active nightlife, and historic sites.

There is no wrong time to visit Rio de Janeiro, whether you are seeking for a beach vacation, a cultural adventure, or a chance to explore the city.

Packing list

Rio de Janeiro Packing List for First-Time Visitors:

Clothes:

• Lightweight, breathable clothing in light colors - Rio has a very hot, humid atmosphere, so you'll want to dress comfortably.

• Good walking shoes - Rio is a highly walk able city, so you'll want to be prepared for long days of touring.

• A few more formal clothing - Rio is a sophisticated city, so pack a few dressier outfits with you for evenings out on the town.

• A hat and sunglasses to keep you cool under the blazing Brazilian heat.

• A light raincoat - in case of unexpected rainfall.

• A swimsuit and a cover-up - for beach days.

Toiletries and Health Products:

• Sunscreen - to protect your skin from the scorching heat of Brazil.

• Insect repellent - to keep annoying mosquitoes at bay.

• A first-aid kit, in case of minor accidents or illnesses.

• Prescription drugs - If you have any long-term health issues, bring your prescription prescriptions with you.

• Personal hygiene goods, such as toothbrushes and toothpaste, shampoo/conditioner, deodorant, and so on.

• If appropriate, feminine hygiene items.

Electricity:

• Camera - to record all of your incredible moments in Rio.

• Laptop - for business or leisure.

• A cell phone and a charger to keep in touch with friends and family back home.

• A portable charger to ensure that your gadgets' batteries don't run out while you're out exploring.

• International plug adapter - for charging your gadgets in various outlets.

Documents:

• Passport - required for entry and exit from Brazil.

• Visa, if necessary.

• Travel insurance paperwork - to ensure you're covered in the event of an emergency.

• Travel and lodging information - to ensure you have all the information you need for your stay in Rio.

Other Items:

• Money - Be sure to carry some local cash with you to utilize in Rio.

• A guidebook to help you discover the greatest locations to visit in the city.

• Personal things - such as jewelry, mementos, or other items you want to bring with you.

• A little backpack in which to carry all of your belongings when out and about.

• A water bottle to keep you hydrated while exploring.

• Travel papers folder - to keep all of your vital paperwork secure and organized throughout your trip.

Chapter 7

EXPLORING RIO DE JANEIRO

Welcome to Rio de Janeiro, the wonderful city! You are in for a wonderful experience as a first-time tourist. The travel to Rio de Janeiro will be memorable. This dynamic city has something for everyone, from its magnificent beaches to its colorful culture and food.

Rio de Janeiro is home to some of the world's most beautiful beaches. The most popular beaches are Copacabana, Ipanema, and Leblon, although there are many more gorgeous beaches to visit.

You'll find what you're searching for in Rio de Janeiro, whether it's a calm beach to rest on or a bustling beach to party on.

Rio de Janeiro's culture is certainly wonderful to witness. The city is a cultural melting pot, and there is never a lack of things to do. There is something for everyone, from touring ancient sites to enjoying the vibrant nightlife.

Rio is also well-known for its delectable gastronomy. Traditional Brazilian delicacies as well as foreign food will tempt your taste buds. You'll be able to find something to fulfill your hunger, whether it's a quick snack or a full-course dinner.

Exploring Rio de Janeiro is an unforgettable experience. With its beautiful beaches, colorful culture, and delectable food, you'll find plenty to enjoy regardless of your interests. So be ready to explore the city and create some unforgettable moments. Have a wonderful time in Rio de Janeiro!

Wildlife

Rio de Janeiro is one of the world's most popular tourist destinations, which is not surprising considering its beautiful beaches, vibrant culture, and incredible wildlife. Rio de Janeiro is filled with life, from the lush Amazon rainforests to the warm Atlantic Rainforest.

Rio de Janeiro is home to a diverse range of species, including monkeys, sloths, and toucans, as well as capybaras, jaguars, and anacondas. Exploring Rio de Janeiro's wildlife may be an exciting experience, whether you're a first-time visitor or a seasoned tourist.

The Amazon Basin is home to some of the world's most varied and distinctive fauna. Although you cannot enter the forest, you may take a boat ride down the River Negro to see the wonderful wildlife that make this location home.

Monkeys, sloths, and toucans are just a few of the spectacular species you'll see on these excursions. You'll also get the opportunity to witness the Amazon's famous pink dolphins.

Another fantastic spot to discover animals in Rio de Janeiro is the Atlantic Rainforest. This complex and unusual habitat is home to a broad range of creatures, including jaguars, ocelots, cougars, and tapirs. There are also many birds, insects, and amphibians to be found here. Hiking on one of the numerous paths in the region is one of the greatest ways to experience the rainforest.

Rio de Janeiro's beaches are also home to some fascinating animals. There's lots to discover when strolling down the dunes, from the brown-throated three-toed sloth to the Brazilian guinea pig. Keep a look out for the green iguana, which may be spotted on the rocks sunning itself.

Lastly, a journey to Rio de Janeiro would be incomplete without a visit to the Tijuca National Park. The gigantic anteater, black-tufted marmoset, and anaconda are among the creatures found in this tropical park. There are also many birds and other species to be found here.

Discovering the animals of Rio de Janeiro may be a very amazing experience. Whether you're a first-time visitor or a seasoned tourist, make time to explore this dynamic city's wonderful wildlife.

The Art

Rio de Janeiro has become worldwide famous for its lively culture, beautiful beaches, and exciting nightlife. This Brazilian city has something for everyone, and this is particularly true when it comes to the cultural sector. Rio de Janeiro offers something for all sorts of art aficionados, from world-class museums to street entertainers.

The Centro Cultural Banco do Brasil (CCBB) is an excellent site to begin your investigation of Rio de Janeiro's cultural scene. This cultural center hosts a wide range of exhibits and activities in the fields of music, theater, dance, and visual arts. There is also a movie theater, a library, and a café.

Another must-see for art aficionados is the Museum of Modern Art of Rio de Janeiro (MAM-Rio), which is situated in the Flamengo area. This museum has an extensive collection of modern art by Brazilian and foreign artists. It also provides a number of educational activities, including workshops, seminars, and courses.

Rio de Janeiro's National Fine Arts Museum (MNBA) is a significant cultural institution. This museum, located in the Botafogo area, includes a permanent collection of Brazilian and foreign art from the 16th century to the present.

During the year, this museum also organizes a range of temporary exhibits and activities.

Theatro Municipal is a historic theatre in the heart of Rio de Janeiro. This magnificent structure was constructed in the early 1900s and has hosted innumerable theater performances, concerts, and other cultural events. The Municipal Theatro has been renovated and is now an important cultural hub in the city.

Rio's streets are also teeming with artists, street performers, and skilled musicians. As you go about the city, you'll see a range of creative people entertaining passers-by. It's a terrific opportunity to immerse yourself in Rio de Janeiro's culture and get a peek of the city's creative energy.

Rio de Janeiro is brimming with art and culture. There is something for everyone in this dynamic and interesting city, whether you are interested in contemporary art, classical music, or street acts. Come experience the arts in Rio de Janeiro; you will not be disappointed.

Luxury Hotels & prices

Rio de Janeiro is one of the world's most beautiful cities and the ideal location for a lavish vacation. It's no surprise that it's one of the world's most popular tourist destinations, with its magnificent beaches, colorful culture, and incredible nightlife.

As a first-time tourist, you will undoubtedly be astonished by the quantity of luxury hotel alternatives available. Here is some information about the greatest luxury hotels in Rio de Janeiro, as well as the pricing you can anticipate to spend.

The Copacabana Palace is one of Rio de Janeiro's most recognizable luxury hotels. This 5-star hotel in the Copacabana district provides magnificent accommodations, great cuisine, and an attractive spa. Hotel costs vary from roughly R$2,400 to R$7,000 per night ($640-$1,850 USD).

The Fasano Rio de Janeiro is an expensive hotel in Rio's fashionable Ipanema area. This hotel exudes opulence while being contemporary, with amenities such as a rooftop pool, gourmet restaurants, and a spa. Hotel costs vary from roughly R$2,000 to R$4,500 per night ($530-$1,200 USD).

Another notable luxury hotel in Rio de Janeiro is the Belmond Copacabana Palace. This 5-star hotel in Copacabana provides stunning views of the ocean and Copacabana beach. Hotel costs vary from roughly R$2,600 to R$6,000 per night ($680-$1,570 USD).

The Sheraton Grand Rio Hotel and Resort is a magnificent hotel in the Barra da Tijuca district of Rio de Janeiro. This hotel has luxurious rooms, a spa, a pool, and many restaurants. Hotel costs vary from roughly R$1,400 to R$3,700 per night ($370-$970 USD).

The Rio Othon Palace is a 5-star hotel in the Copacabana area of Rio de Janeiro. This hotel has luxurious accommodations, a spa, a pool, many restaurants, and an amazing view of Copacabana Beach. Hotel costs vary from roughly R$1,600 to R$4,000 per night ($420-$1,050 USD).

These are only a handful of Rio de Janeiro's numerous luxury hotels. Costs may vary based on the season and any special deals that are available. While selecting a hotel, keep your budget in mind as well as the services that each hotel provides. Whichever hotel you choose, you will have a wonderful vacation in Rio de Janeiro!

Stunning Beaches

Rio de Janeiro is a beautiful city noted for its beautiful beaches. Rio de Janeiro offers something for everyone, from the famed Copacabana to the lesser-known Prainha and Grumari.

Whether you wish to relax on the beach or participate in some of the city's thrilling activities and attractions, these beaches will make your first visit to Rio de Janeiro a memorable experience.

•Copacabana is Rio de Janeiro's most well-known beach. It is a 4-kilometer strip of white sand surrounded by palm trees and peppered with beach bars, restaurants, and shops. It is one of the city's most popular beaches and a terrific location to unwind and soak up the rays. Volleyball, soccer, jet skiing, and parasailing are among the sports and attractions available at the beach.

•Ipanema: This beach, situated close to Copacabana, is one of Rio de Janeiro's most elite. It attracts the city's rich and celebrities and is noted for its stylish beach bars, restaurants, and shopping. It also hosts a number of activities, including volleyball, surfing, and kite surfing.

•Prainha: This little beach between Copacabana and Ipanema is ideal for those seeking a more isolated beach experience. Prainha is recognized for its beautiful mountain vistas as well as its pure waters, which are ideal for swimming and snorkeling.

•Grumari: Grumari is a beautiful beach in Rio de Janeiro's southern region. It is an excellent location for anyone seeking to escape the rush and bustle of the city and discover the gorgeous coastline landscape. The beach is renowned for surfing, kite surfing, and windsurfing due to its crystal blue seas.

•Barra da Tijuca: This beautiful beach is situated in the western portion of Rio de Janeiro and is one of the city's longest. It is an excellent place for individuals wishing to rest because of its serene and tranquil ambience. It also has a number of sports and attractions, including volleyball, kayaking, and windsurfing.

These are just a handful of the beautiful beaches in Rio de Janeiro. Whichever style of beach experience you want, you will undoubtedly find it in this lovely city. So, take your sunscreen and prepare to tour some of the world's greatest beaches.

Finest Museums

Rio de Janeiro is one of the world's most dynamic and attractive cities, with breathtaking beaches, renowned buildings, and a distinct culture that make it a must-see vacation. It also has some of the top museums in the world, providing an excellent chance to learn about the city's rich tradition and culture. For first-time visitors to Rio de Janeiro, these are some of the best museums to see.

The National Museum of Brazil is the oldest and biggest museum in Brazil, as well as one of the most significant in South America. Almost 20,000 objects from throughout the globe are included in the collection, ranging from pre-Columbian antiquities to modern art. There is also a large library and an auditorium.

The Imperial Palace Museum: Formerly the residence of the Brazilian royal family, this museum provides tourists with an insight into the country's imperial history. There are royal furniture, jewels, and artworks in the collection.

The Museum of Modern Art: This museum includes an extraordinary collection of works by some of the world's top modern and contemporary artists, including Pablo Picasso, Gustav Klimt, and Gustav Klimt. There is also a library and an auditorium.

The National History Museum is devoted to Brazil's history, containing exhibits on the country's indigenous inhabitants, colonial era, and independence. It also has an excellent collection of pre-Columbian antiquities.

The Museum of Indian Art has a huge collection of items from Brazil's indigenous people. It also has an interactive exhibit on the country's indigenous cultures and history.

The National Museum of Natural History: This museum has a vast collection of plant and animal species, as well as minerals, fossils, and pre-Columbian artifacts. There is also a library and an auditorium.

The Museum of Contemporary Art: This museum contains a diverse collection of modern and contemporary art by some of the world's most well-known artists. There is also a library and an auditorium.

The National Maritime Museum is devoted to the history of Brazil's nautical culture, featuring exhibits on ships, navigation, and marine commerce. There is also a library and an auditorium.

The Museum of Fine Arts: This museum includes a remarkable collection of works by well-known painters like as Rembrandt, Monet, and Picasso. There is also a library and an auditorium.

The National Science and Technology Museum: This museum has a variety of scientific and technology displays, including interactive exhibits on astronomy, biology, chemistry, and physics. There is also a library and an auditorium.

Whatever your hobbies are, there is certain to be a museum in Rio de Janeiro that will pique your curiosity and deliver a unique experience. Hence, throughout your vacation, be sure to spend some time exploring the city's amazing museums.

Best Shopping Mall

Rio de Janeiro is a bustling city brimming with culture and vitality, and the shopping experience is no exception. Rio de Janeiro, being one of the world's major shopping destinations, provides tourists with a plethora of options for retail therapy. Rio has everything for everyone, from high-end luxury stores to street markets.

First-time visitors to Rio should go to Barra Shopping, the city's biggest and most contemporary retail complex, for the ultimate shopping experience.

Barra Shopping, located in the upscale Barra da Tijuca neighborhood, is stretched over many floors and has over 400 businesses. It's ideal for picking up designer labels, as well as high-street and local businesses.

Barra Shopping has various world-renowned brands, like Louis Vuitton, Gucci, and Prada, if you're seeking for luxury products. There are also various jewelry and watch boutiques that sell unique items.

For those on a tight budget, the mall also contains a variety of retailers selling lower-priced products, including H&M, Zara, and Riachuelo. There are also a few electronics outlets where you can purchase anything from phones and tablets to cameras and computers.

The mall also features a diverse assortment of restaurants, pubs, and cafés serving a variety of foreign cuisines. Several of these restaurants have outside dining with views of the beach and lagoon.

Barra Shopping also contains a 12-screen cinema, bowling alley, and ice rink. A big gaming arcade with a laser tag area is also available.

Barra Shopping is ideal for first-time visitors to Rio de Janeiro because to its wide variety of retailers, food choices, and entertainment.

Nightclubs and Bar

Rio de Janeiro is gradually becoming a popular tourist destination in South America and is a fantastic spot to spend a night out. The city has a bustling environment, and one of the primary attractions for travelers is its nightlife.

Rio de Janeiro offers something for everyone, whether you want a low-key pub, a chic nightclub, or a noisy after-hours venue.

If you're seeking for a terrific bar experience, Rio de Janeiro has lots to offer. The city has a broad range of pubs, from refined cocktail lounges to vibrant sports bars. Some of Rio de Janeiro's most popular bars are Bar do Mineiro, Bar do Arco, and Bar do Copa. These bars provide a broad variety of beverages as well as a fun environment for a night out.

Rio de Janeiro features several terrific nightclubs for those searching for a more high-energy experience. The city is home to some of South America's best clubs, including the world-famous Fosfobox. This club has a combination of electronic music, live music, and DJs. Some renowned Rio de Janeiro nightclubs include La Paz, Club 00, and La Favela.

Rio de Janeiro also offers several amazing alternatives for after-hours entertainment. There are several clubs and pubs operating into the early hours of the morning. These clubs are an excellent way to continue the party after the conventional clubs have closed. Kuka, Black Jack, and The Week are some of the most popular after-hours places.

Whichever style of nightlife experience you want, Rio de Janeiro offers something for everyone. From refined cocktail bars to exciting after-hours locations, the city is brimming with amazing bars and clubs. Rio de Janeiro, with its dynamic atmosphere and active nightlife, is an excellent destination to sample the finest of South America's nightlife.

Festival & Entertainments

Rio de Janeiro, one of the world's most lively cities, is famous for its breathtaking natural beauty, vibrant culture, and spectacular festivals and entertainment. As a first-time visitor, you will be astounded by the many festivals and events that take place throughout the year. Rio de Janeiro has something for everyone, from the world-renowned Carnival to the spectacular New Year's Eve fireworks extravaganza.

The world-famous Carnival is one of Rio de Janeiro's most popular celebrations. Carnival, which takes place every February, is famed for its bright parades, boisterous music, and brilliant costumes.

The primary attraction is the Sambadrome parade, which displays some of the most beautiful floats and costumes from all over the globe. During Carnival, you may also enjoy the street celebrations known as blocos that take place around the city.

The New Year's Eve fireworks show is another famous event in Rio de Janeiro. This event takes place along Copacabana Beach and boasts a spectacular fireworks show that lights up the sky. It is one of the year's most stunning spectacles, attracting hundreds of thousands of people.

There are other additional events in Rio de Janeiro throughout the year. The Festival de Diablos, the International Street Fair, the Rock in Rio Music Festival, and the Bienal de Artes Visuais are among these festivities. For tourists, each of these events offers something distinct and fascinating.

Rio de Janeiro has some of the top entertainment options in the world. You may see some of the city's best musicians, dancers, and theatrical troupes perform.

The city also has some of the world's greatest nightlife, including pubs, clubs, and live music venues. There are also some of the top restaurants in town, dishing up delectable delicacies from all over the globe.

In summary, Rio de Janeiro has some of the world's top festivals and entertainment. As a first-time visitor, you will be astounded by the vitality and enthusiasm of this incredible city. Rio de Janeiro offers something for everyone, whether you're searching for a wonderful event to attend or a memorable experience.

Flowing waterfalls

Rio de Janeiro is a wonderful Brazilian city noted for its magnificent beaches and environment. The city's many waterfalls are one of its most prominent attractions. These water waterfalls, which are typically surrounded by thick greenery, create a lovely scene for tourists to enjoy.

Cascatinha Taunay is Rio de Janeiro's most popular waterfall. This waterfall is located in the heart of Tijuca National Park and is one of the city's most popular attractions. The water rushes down a sheer rock wall, giving tourists a beautiful perspective of the surrounding landscape.

Tourists may walk to the waterfall or take a boat excursion on the adjoining Lagoa Rodrigo de Freitas.

Another renowned waterfall in Rio de Janeiro is the Salto de Itacolomi. This spectacular waterfall is found in Itacolomi State Park and is home to a wide range of vegetation and wildlife.

Because of the area's high cliffs and rocks, it's also a favorite place for rock climbers. Tourists may obtain a better perspective of the waterfall by taking a boat trip on the neighboring Lagoa Rodrigo de Freitas.

Another stunning waterfall in Rio de Janeiro is the Cachoeira da Lapa. This magnificent waterfall is situated in Tijuca National Park and is one of the tallest in the area.

Due to its spectacular views and closeness to the city center, it is also one of the most frequented locations in the city. Tourists may obtain a better perspective of the waterfall by taking a boat trip on the neighboring Lagoa Rodrigo de Freitas.

Cachoeira do Horto is Rio de Janeiro's fourth most popular waterfall. This waterfall is nestled amid the rich flora of the Horto Florestal National Park. Tourists may stroll to the waterfall or take a boat trip on adjacent Lagoa Rodrigo de Freitas for a better perspective.

These are just a few of the waterfalls that can be seen in Rio de Janeiro. Whether you are a first-time visitor to the city or a seasoned tourist, the waterfalls of Rio de Janeiro will give you with a memorable experience.

Explore the jungles

The world's jungles are among the most unique, interesting, and mysterious areas on the planet. They are home to plants and species found nowhere else in the globe, and visiting a jungle may be one of life's most remarkable experiences.

Before heading into the forest, first-time tourists should be prepared and know what to anticipate.

First and foremost, ensure that you have the proper gear, supplies, and equipment for your jungle excursion. Since the humidity in the jungle may be intense, you'll want to wear lightweight and breathable clothes to keep your body heat as low as possible.

You should also pack a hat and sunglasses to protect yourself from the sun, as well as insect repellant to keep troublesome pests at bay. You should also have lots of water and food, as well as a first aid kit in case of medical issues.

It is also critical to be mindful of the jungle's possible risks. Several creatures, such as snakes and wild cats, may be deadly, so it is essential to be cautious and respect their area. Also, you should be mindful of the terrain, since it may be rather difficult, and you should wear appropriate hiking shoes.

Another critical part of going into the bush is having an experienced guide. A guide can show you the finest paths, assist you in navigating the terrain, and point out animals and other noteworthy sites.

Ultimately, it is critical to respect the forest and its people. Never touch or disturb any plants or animals, and always dispose of garbage or rubbish in the right locations.

Touring a jungle may be a memorable experience and an excellent opportunity to learn more about the world's natural beauties.

" With proper planning, you can guarantee that your jungle expedition is both safe and entertaining".

Chapter 8

PRIMARY NEEDS

Accommodation

Rio de Janeiro is an interesting and energetic city that attracts people from all over the globe. Whether you're traveling for the first time or returning for another adventure, there are lots of places to stay.

The city has something for everyone's budget and taste, so you'll have no difficulty finding something that suits you. These are some of the most popular Rio de Janeiro lodging alternatives for first-time travelers.

Hotels: There is a vast range of hotels in Rio de Janeiro, from budget-friendly alternatives to opulent five-star resorts. The Copacabana Palace, the Sheraton Rio Hotel & Resort, and the Windsor Miramar are among the city's most popular hotels.

They all provide exceptional facilities and services, making them a wonderful option for any tourist.

Hostels: Hostels are a terrific way to save money while still having a great time in Rio de Janeiro. Hostels are typically dormitory-style lodgings with shared facilities, but they sometimes provide other amenities such as kitchens and lounges and may be a fantastic way to meet other travelers.

The Rio Hostel, the Rio International Hostel, and the Urca Beach Hostel are among the most popular hostels in Rio de Janeiro.

Apartments: If you want a more private and home-like setting, you may rent an apartment in Rio de Janeiro. Apartments come in a variety of sizes and types, and they may be leased for a short or lengthy period of time. Airbnb, Rio Apartment Rentals, and ViviRio are among the most popular rental firms in the city.

Bed & Breakfasts: Bed & Breakfasts are an excellent choice for guests seeking a more personalized and home-style experience in Rio de Janeiro. These lodgings usually include a private room, a communal bathroom, and breakfast. Casa do Lago, Casa do Mar, and Casa das Acacias are among the city's most popular B&Bs.

There is an accommodation choice in Rio de Janeiro for everyone, regardless of price or tastes. With so many alternatives, you'll be able to choose the ideal spot to stay.

Restaurants

Rio de Janeiro is one of the world's most popular tourist attractions. It's no surprise that many people come to enjoy the city's distinctive atmosphere, given its lively culture and breathtaking environment.

While visiting Rio, there are several restaurants to select from, each with its own unique offering. There's something for everyone, whether you want a traditional Brazilian feast or foreign food.

If you want to have a true Brazilian experience, go to one of the numerous churrascarias. These establishments specialize on grilled meats, often served on skewers and accompanied by rice, beans, and farofa (a toasted flour dish).

Choose one of Rio's numerous fine dining venues for a more affluent experience. You'll discover a wide range of foreign and regional specialties, as well as some of the greatest wines in town, here.

If you're looking for something more informal, visit one of the city's numerous cafés and botequins. These venues are often tiny and personal, making them ideal for relaxing and enjoying some good meals. Several of these cafés offer traditional Brazilian foods like feijoada (a black bean stew) and acarajé (acarajé is a kind of acarajé) (a fried shrimp dish).

If you want to have a good time, you should go to one of the city's numerous pubs or nightclubs. There's some amazing music, dancing, and beverages here. Several of the bars also provide food, so you can eat something while you're out.

Whatever you're searching for, Rio de Janeiro is guaranteed to have something to suit you. There's something for everyone among its many restaurants, cafés, and pubs. So go out there and enjoy the cuisine and atmosphere of this lovely city!

Activities

1. **See the Christ the Redeemer Statue:** For stunning views of the city, go to the famed 130-foot monument of Jesus Christ atop Corcovado Mountain.

2. **Visit Copacabana Beach:**which has white sand and azure waves and is one of the world's most renowned beaches.

3. **Take a Sugarloaf Mountain Tour:** Soak in the breathtaking views of Rio from the peak of Sugarloaf Mountain, which has a cable car journey to the top.

4. **Shop at Feira de So Cristóvo:** Learn about the local culture at this big market that sells everything from food to crafts.

5. Take a walk along the colorful stairs of world-renowned artist Jorge Selarón, a dedication to the people of Rio.

6. **Visit the Botanical Garden:** Enjoy the city's biggest botanical garden's magnificent gardens, waterfalls, and pathways.

7. **Hiking in Tijuca National Park:** Walk through the world's biggest urban jungle at Tijuca National Park.

8. **Visit Lapa and Santa Teresa:** Go through these ancient areas that are rich in culture, art, and music.

9. **Taste Local Cuisine**: Try some of Rio's delectable, fresh seafood and other traditional delicacies.

10. **Check Out the Nightlife**: Enjoy Rio's exciting nightlife, which includes several pubs, clubs, and lounges.

Tour Packages

Rio de Janeiro, sometimes known as the "Marvelous City," is one of Brazil's most famous tourist attractions. Rio de Janeiro has something for everyone, with its beautiful beaches, rich culture, and thrilling nightlife.

Rio de Janeiro, from the renowned Christ the Redeemer monument to the gorgeous Sugarloaf Mountain, provides a wealth of sights and activities, making it a perfect holiday destination.

When it comes to booking a trip package, Rio de Janeiro has several possibilities. There is something for every style of visitor, from classic sightseeing trips to more adventurous adventures.

These are some of the most popular tour packages in Rio de Janeiro:

City Tour: If you want to obtain a complete perspective of Rio de Janeiro, a city tour is the way to go. Most city tour packages include stops at popular sights like the Christ the Redeemer monument and Sugarloaf Mountain, as well as excursions in some of Rio's most famous districts like Copacabana and Santa Teresa.

Rio de Janeiro is the ideal place for a beach trip due to its vast length of stunning beaches. Stops to some of the city's most popular beaches, such as Ipanema and Copacabana, are common on beach excursions. Some beach cruises include visits to neighbouring islands like Ilha Grande.

Rio de Janeiro is a fantastic location for anyone seeking an adrenaline rush. Rappelling, rafting, motorcycling, and hiking are common activities on adventure vacations. Visits to surrounding national parks and jungles, such as Tijuca National Park, are also included in some adventure excursions.

Culinary Tour: If you want to sample Rio de Janeiro's delectable food, a culinary tour is the way to go. Culinary tours sometimes include stops at some of the city's most prominent restaurants as well as stops at local markets and food booths.

Nightlife Tour: Rio de Janeiro is well-known for its active nightlife, and a nightlife tour is an excellent opportunity to sample it. Nightlife excursions usually include stops at some of the city's most popular pubs and nightclubs, as well as live music venues.

Rio de Janeiro provides something for everyone, no matter what style of travel package you're searching for.

Electric plugs

Rio de Janeiro uses the Brazilian standard of 110 volts and 60 hertz, with plugs with two circular pins. Since the plugs are identical to those used in the United States and Canada, North American appliances may be plugged straight into the wall outlets.

Travelers from other countries, on the other hand, should pack a travel adapter to suit the local sockets.

The plugs and sockets used in Rio de Janeiro are generally the same as those used across Brazil.

Chapter 9

SURVIVAL GUIDE

This survival guide will assist you in making the most of your time in Rio and ensuring that your stay is safe, entertaining, and unforgettable.

Rio de Janeiro is nicknamed as the "Cidade Maravilhosa," and it's simple to understand why. Rio is a city of miracles, from the famed Christ the Redeemer monument to the magnificent beaches of Ipanema and Copacabana.

But it's also worth noting that Rio can be a hazardous city, particularly for the inexperienced. That is why it is critical to empower oneself with the information and skills necessary to be safe and have a good time in Rio.

This chapter will teach you all you need to know about making the most of your stay in Rio. We'll also provide you some useful tips, tactics, and advice to help you make the most of your stay in the Marvelous City.

Therefore, without further ado, let's get started with our Rio de Janeiro survival guide for first-time travelers!

Take care of your passport

1. Keep your passport in a safe place. Keep it in a secure location, such as a hotel room safe or an airport locker. Don't keep it out in the open in your hotel room or while you're out and about.

2. Make several copies of your passport. Make at least two copies of your passport before leaving. One should be left with a trusted friend or family member, while the other should be brought with you.

3. Remember to carry your passport. Always have your passport on you at all times. If you are leaving the country, bring it with you when you go through customs.

4. Confirm that your passport is still valid. Before you go, double-check the expiry date on your passport. Several nations require you to have a passport that is valid for at least six months after your intended stay.

5. Report a lost or stolen passport. If your passport is lost or stolen, notify the local police as well as the closest consulate or embassy. This will assist you in obtaining a new passport.

Learn basic Portuguese language phrases

1. Begin by learning some fundamental greetings. While learning any language, greetings are essential. "Oi!" is a common Portuguese greeting.

2. Learn some fundamental Portuguese phrases to get you started in a discussion. "Como vai?" is one example. (How are you?) "Where do you live?" (Where do you live?) and "What is your name?" (Can you tell me your name?

3. Study the fundamentals of Portuguese grammar. Understanding the fundamentals of Portuguese language will allow you to speak more successfully. Portuguese nouns, for example, have gender and may be masculine or feminine.

Understanding how to modify a word's ending to fit the gender of the noun will help you speak more effectively.

4. Get some practice with a native speaker. One of the most effective methods to learn Portuguese is to practice with a native speaker. You may learn a language by using internet resources or by finding a language exchange partner.

5. Make use of flashcards. Flashcards are an excellent tool for learning new words and phrases. On one side, write the Portuguese term and on the other, the English translation. You may also practice verb conjugations using flashcards.

6. Listen to and watch Portuguese music and movies. Listening to Portuguese music and seeing Portuguese movies might help you learn the language quickly. It will assist you in becoming acquainted with the pronunciation as well as learning some slang vocabulary.

7. Read books and newspapers in Portuguese. Reading books and newspapers in Portuguese is an excellent approach to learn the language. It will assist you in becoming acquainted with the grammar as well as learning new vocabulary terms.

Get used to local transportation system

1. Get acquainted with the various modes of transportation accessible to you. Buses, trams, trains, taxis, and ride-sharing services are examples of public transportation.

2. Determine the most cost-effective and convenient mode of transportation. Consider getting a tourist ticket that provides unrestricted public transit access.

3. Plan your route ahead of time and double-check schedules to guarantee you get on time at your destination.

4. Get acquainted with the regulations and practices of local public transit. Pay attention to announcements and be kind to other passengers.

5. Have a map or trip planner accessible in case you get disoriented.

6. Be mindful of your surroundings and safeguard your things.

7. If you want assistance, ask the locals.

Avoid traveling alone at night

Going alone in new locations especially at night in Rio de Janeiro may be risky. Rio de Janeiro is a huge and busy city, thus there are several locations that visitors should avoid. The city is notorious for its high levels of crime and violence, so you should take care to secure your safety.

While traveling alone in Rio de Janeiro, it is vital to remain in well-lit, busy areas, particularly at night. Avoid taking shortcuts and walking at night, since they might put you at risk. If you must go out at night, utilize public transit or a cab, and never walk alone.

If you must walk, do it in a group and be mindful of your surroundings at all times. Going to unexpected places or taking unusual routes might be perilous. It is also important to dress modestly and avoid wearing dazzling or costly jewelry.

It is also important to understand the local culture and traditions. Follow local laws and respect local culture, even if it differs from yours. Keep an eye out for local gangs and potentially risky regions.

Apart from being secure when traveling alone in Rio de Janeiro, it is essential to take steps to safeguard yourself and your things. Keep your passport, money, and other critical papers in a safe location at all times. Consider bringing a photocopy of your passport and leaving the original in the hotel safe.

Lastly, being connected when traveling alone in Rio de Janeiro is critical. Make sure you have a functional phone with a local number and a method to contact relatives and friends in the event of an emergency.

Traveling alone in Rio de Janeiro may be a rewarding and interesting experience. Nonetheless, taking the essential steps to safeguard your safety and well-being is critical. Keep an eye on your surroundings and take the appropriate precautions to keep yourself and your stuff safe.

Be aware of pickpockets and other street crime

Rio de Janeiro is one of the world's most popular tourist destinations. Regrettably, it is also well-known for its pick pocketing and street violence.

Pick pocketing is a serious problem in Rio de Janeiro, so take measures and be alert of your surroundings.

Pickpockets often prey on visitors and the unwary in congested locations such as Metro stations, public transit, retail malls, beaches, tourist sites, and busy streets.

They often operate in groups of two or more and might be difficult to detect. Pick pocketing is most often associated with the theft of wallets, handbags, mobile phones, and other electronic items.

It is important to remain aware of your surroundings at all times and to keep your possessions near to you. It's also a good idea not to wear costly jewelry or carry significant quantities of cash.

Keep your passport and other critical papers in a secure location as well. While utilizing public transit, it is equally crucial to remain vigilant of your surroundings and suspicious behavior.

Several types of street crime exist in Rio de Janeiro, in addition to pick pocketing. Muggings, purse snatching, carjackings, and assaults are all common crimes. To prevent being a victim of a crime, it is essential to be aware of your surroundings and to take the appropriate safeguards.

While visiting Rio de Janeiro, it is essential to remain in well-lit and secure places. Whenever possible, avoid walking alone at night and instead use a cab or public transit. It is also important to be aware of your surroundings and to follow your instincts if anything does not seem right.

Generally, it is essential to be aware of the possible threats of pick pocketing and street crime in Rio de Janeiro. You may considerably lower your chances of being a victim of a crime by taking the essential measures and being aware of your surroundings.

Avoid carrying large amounts of cash

First-time travelers to Rio de Janeiro should avoid carrying huge sums of cash. This is because of the city's high crime rate and the chance of being targeted by pickpockets or opportunistic thieves.

Visitors should spend cash carefully and withdraw monies as required using credit cards or ATM cards. Guests should also be vigilant of their surroundings and personal possessions at all times.

Take extra precautions when using ATM

1. Be mindful of your surroundings and avoid using ATM in remote or dark locations.

2. Do not utilize computers that look to have been tampered with or otherwise destroyed.

3. Avoid using ATM if there is a significant crowd present.

4. Be wary of pickpockets and keep your PIN number safe.

5. Only use ATM throughout the day.

6. Check to see whether your credit/debit card has a chip reader.

7. Use ATM situated inside banks whenever feasible.

8. Before leaving the ATM, double-check that the transaction is complete and that you have got your cash.

9. Avoid carrying significant sums of money.

10. Keep track of all your transactions and review your bank statements on a regular basis.

Research your accommodation options in advance

Studying lodging alternatives ahead of time is a wonderful method to guarantee that you receive the greatest bargain and the best experience possible when traveling. While evaluating various possibilities, it is important to evaluate variables such as location, pricing, facilities, and reviews.

Preparing ahead of time assists you to make an educated choice and prevent any last-minute shocks. Moreover, investigating your lodging alternatives might help you discover hidden treasures and one-of-a-kind experiences that you would not have discovered otherwise.

Have travel insurance in case of an emergency

For first-time travelers to Rio de Janeiro, travel insurance is strongly advised. It is essential that you have coverage for medical expenditures, lost baggage, trip cancellation, and other unforeseen circumstances. Search for a policy that offers medical evacuation coverage, as well as emergency medical care in Brazil. Read the tiny print of any insurance you buy to ensure that it matches your requirements.

Tips to make new friends

1. Enroll in a Portuguese language class. Even if you simply learn a few words, it will make it easier to converse with people and create new acquaintances.

2. Go out and about in the city. Rio de Janeiro is full with incredible sights and activities, and getting to know the city is a terrific opportunity to meet new people.

3. Participate in community activities. Rio has a plethora of events such as concerts, festivals, and cultural events, all of which provide excellent opportunity to meet new people.

4. Participate in a local sports team or club. Whether you like football or yoga, there are several teams and sessions where you may meet individuals who share your interests.

5. Visit the beach. Rio's beaches are ideal for meeting new people as well as relaxing and admiring the city's natural beauty.

6. Use internet resources. There are several internet tools, such as Meetup and Couch surfing, that may assist you in finding folks to hang out with in Rio.

Chapter 10

HIDDEN GEMS TO EXPLORE

Vista Chinesa

Vista Chinesa is a mountain top in the Brazilian city of Rio de Janeiro. It is the city's third tallest mountain, standing at 722 meters. Vista Chinesa provides breathtaking views of the city, neighboring hills, and the Atlantic Ocean.

The top may be reached from the Parque Nacional da Tijuca, a vast natural reserve in Rio de Janeiro's center. Visitors to the park may ride the cable car to the summit or climb up the mountain. The trek is rather straightforward and takes around 1.5 hours to reach the peak. There are various observation sites along the path that provide breathtaking views of the city and neighboring environs.

Vista Chinesa offers a panoramic view of Rio de Janeiro and the neighboring hills. Photographers and visitors flock here to capture images of the city and its famed attractions, such as the Christ the Redeemer monument, Sugarloaf Mountain, and the beaches of Copacabana and Ipanema.

Birdwatchers flock to Vista Chinesa as well. Toucans, parrots, macaws, and hummingbirds are among the numerous bird species found in the region. Several tiny creatures, such as capybaras and raccoons, live on the top.

Vista Chinesa is an excellent day excursion from Rio de Janeiro. The views from the summit are spectacular, and the trek is a fantastic chance to get some exercise while still enjoying the fresh air. Vista Chinesa is well worth a visit, whether you're a photographer, birdwatcher, or just seeking for a lovely view.

Jardim Botânico

The Jardim Botânico (Botanical Garden) is a public park in Rio de Janeiro, Brazil. It is one of the city's oldest parks, having been established in 1808, and is home to over 6,000 plant varieties, many of which are endemic to Brazil.

It also serves as a haven for a variety of birds, butterflies, and other species. There is a big lake in the park, as well as various gardens and a library. Jardim Botânico is a renowned tourist location that organizes a range of events throughout the year.

Museu de Arte Contemporânea

The Museu de Arte Contemporânea (MuseuMAC) is a contemporary art museum in Niterói, Brazil. It was created in 1996 by famous Brazilian architect Oscar Niemeyer and inaugurated in 1996.

The museum focuses on contemporary art and has a permanent collection of works by Brazilian and international artists.

The structure is regarded as one of Niemeyer's masterpieces and is notable for its distinctive design. It is made up of two circular buildings joined by a walkway that provides tourists with views of Guanabara Bay.

There is also an auditorium, a library, and a café in the museum. The MuseuMAC organizes a number of exhibits as well as educational events like as talks, seminars, and lessons. In addition, the museum supports an artist residency program that permits artists to work and live at the museum for a period of time.

Parque Lage

Parque Lage is a public park in the Brazilian city of Rio de Janeiro. The park is situated in the city center and is a popular attraction for both residents and visitors.

It is located on a hill with breathtaking views of Guanabara Bay, Corcovado, and Sugarloaf Peak. The park has a huge area with gardens, lagoons, and lakes, as well as a diverse range of flora and animals.

A historic house, which is now a museum and art school, is also located in the park. A rich businessman erected the home in the 1920s, and it is now a cultural icon. Guests may have a picnic, take a leisurely walk, or explore the park's various attractions.

The quiet environment and spectacular vistas make Parque Lage a favorite destination for families and couples.

Praia Vermelha

Praia Vermelha (Red Beach) is a Brazilian beach situated just south of Rio de Janeiro. It is one of the most popular beaches in the region, recognized for its beautiful ocean vistas and brilliant red sand.

A variety of species, including sea turtles and seagulls, may be seen on the beach. The beach is ideal for swimming, sunbathing, and resting. Tourists may also explore the adjacent trails and enjoy the breathtaking views from the cliffs. Surfing and kite surfing are among popular sports in Praia Vermelha.

Pedra da Gávea

Pedra da Gávea is a massive monolith in Rio de Janeiro, Brazil's Tijuca Forest. It is the highest point in the city, standing at 842 meters (2,762 feet). It is a famous hiking and natural attraction, and it is widely regarded as one of the city's most prominent emblems.

The name "Pedra da Gávea" refers to the mountain's form, which resembles an upturned boat (a "gávea" in Portuguese).

The peak of Pedra da Gávea provides a panoramic view of Rio de Janeiro, including the urban area, beaches, and other mountains. The journey to the summit is difficult and needs some basic climbing abilities.

A network of routes leads to the peak, but the most famous approach is the "Via Ferrata," a steep, exposed route with iron rungs, cables, and ladders. The climb usually takes 3-4 hours, depending on the difficulty level.

The region around Pedra da Gávea's top is home to several bird and animal species, and the views of the surrounding forest and city are stunning. The ascent to the peak is a unique experience that many people will remember for many years.

Parque Nacional da Tijuca

The Parque Nacional da Tijuca is a national park in Rio de Janeiro, Brazil. It is the world's biggest urban forest, covering 32 km2. The park, which was founded in 1961, is home to many endangered species, including the golden lion tamarin and the endangered Atlantic Forest flora.

The Tijuca Forest, which is home to a multitude of waterfalls and trails, as well as the famed Christ the Redeemer monument, are among the attractions in Park Nacional da Tijuca. Hiking, bird viewing, rock climbing, and camping are among the activities available at the park.

The park also has a variety of cultural attractions, including the Escadaria Selarón, a stairway adorned with tiles from all over the globe, and the Museu de Arte do Rio, which exhibits Brazilian art and culture.

The Park Nacional da Tijuca is a renowned tourist attraction as well as an essential component of Brazilian culture. UNESCO has also classified it as a World Heritage Site.

Museu de Arte do Rio

Museu de Arte do Rio (MAR) is a Brazilian art museum in Rio de Janeiro. It was founded in 2013 as a collaboration between the Rio de Janeiro State Government, the Rio de Janeiro Institute of Art and Culture, and the Federal University of Rio de Janeiro.

The museum is situated in the renovated Palace of the Counts of Pinhal, a neoclassical structure in Rio de Janeiro's downtown region. The museum has a permanent collection of almost 5,000 pieces of art dating from the 16th century to the present. It also hosts a variety of temporary exhibits, educational programs, and cultural events.

The museum's purpose is to offer a platform for debate, study, and contemplation while promoting Rio de Janeiro's art and culture.

Museu Histórico Nacional

The Museu Histórico Nacional (National Historical Museum) is a Brazilian history museum situated in the historic district of Quinta da Boa Vista in Rio de Janeiro.

The Brazilian government established the museum in 1922, making it one of the country's oldest. It is the official depository for historical items and documentation from Brazil.

The museum holds a huge collection of papers, artifacts, and artefacts relating to Brazilian history from the early colonial era to the current day. It contains paintings, sculptures, coins, furniture, ceramics, musical instruments, and textiles, as well as records relating to significant historical events.

It also has a library filled with literature on Brazilian history and culture.

Visitors may participate in educational events and activities such as lectures, seminars, and guided tours at the museum.

It also serves as a venue for temporary exhibits and cultural activities. The museum is available to the public and entry is free.

Quinta da Boa Vista

Quinta da Boa Vista is a big public park in the Brazilian city of Rio de Janeiro. The park, located on the city's northern outskirts, is one of the world's biggest urban parks.

The park spans approximately 1,400 acres (570 hectares) and includes a zoo, a botanical garden, a castle, and various monuments.

The park's history stretches back to the late 18th century, when King John VI of Portugal authorized the building of a palace on the grounds of what is now the park, known as the Quinta da Boa Vista.

The palace was finished in 1822 and served as the Portuguese royal family's vacation retreat until the monarchy was dissolved in 1889.

The palace was then utilized as a presidential home and then as a military school until being turned into a museum in 1945. The palace now contains a variety of historical exhibitions, as well as a library and a theater.

The park also has a zoo, which was founded in 1945 and now houses over 1,600 species from all over the globe. The zoo comprises mammals, birds, reptiles, amphibians, and fishes, as well as an aquarium and a butterfly house.

The botanical garden, which has over 2,000 varieties of plants from throughout the globe, is also a popular feature in the park. Monuments, fountains, and a variety of leisure places are among the other attractions in the park.

Chapter 11

HEALTH & SECURITY

Rio de Janeiro is one of the most recognizable cities in the world, and it has a lot to offer in terms of health and security. The city is well-known for its lively culture, beautiful beaches, and thick jungle.

It is also a major commercial and tourist centre, and it has made significant efforts to emphasize the health and safety of its inhabitants and visitors.

The government has created a comprehensive system of public healthcare and social assistance programs, as well as a variety of security measures, including 24-hour surveillance, CCTV monitoring, and a strong police presence.

The city also has a variety of specialized security units committed to combating crime and safeguarding the public. Moreover, Rio de Janeiro is home to a variety of public health organizations and projects, such as the Rio de Janeiro Health Department and the Brazilian Association for Mental Health.

The city is dedicated to creating a safe and secure environment for all of its people and visitors via the implementation of these programs.

Health Capacity

Rio de Janeiro has a considerable ability to care for its residents' health. Hundreds of governmental and private hospitals, clinics, and other health facilities can be found throughout the city.

There are also several health facilities, some of which specialize on certain illnesses or health problems. Moreover, the municipal administration has invested significantly in health infrastructure, including the building of new facilities and the expansion of existing ones.

These expenditures have enhanced the quality of care offered to people and helped to minimize appointment and treatment wait times.

Health insurance

Rio de Janeiro is the second most populous city in Brazil and one of the most visited cities in the world. Health insurance is available in Rio de Janeiro from a variety of insurance carriers and is available to both locals and visitors.

The Brazilian government provides universal health care to all Brazilian citizens, regardless of income, under the Sistema Unico de Saude (SUS). SUS provides free preventive and curative health care, including hospitalizations, surgeries, and medications.

Private health insurance is also available in Rio de Janeiro and may be a realistic option for those seeking more comprehensive coverage than SUS. Private health insurance coverage often cover doctor and hospital visits, as well as prescription medications, and provide access to a greater range of health-care services.

Organizations such as Projeto Saude and Saude Sem Fronteiras provide health care services to disadvantaged communities in Rio de Janeiro for those who do not qualify for SUS or private health insurance. These organizations give free or low-cost medical services and drugs to those in need.

Health facilities

In Rio de Janeiro, there are several public and private healthcare institutions, including hospitals, clinics, health centers, and specialty centers.

<u>Hospitals that are open to the public</u>

Rio de Janeiro has a number of public hospitals

Municipal Health Department of Rio de Janeiro

Hospital Municipal Souza Aguiar

Hospital Municipal Miguel Couto,

Hospital Municipal dos Servidores do Estado

Hospital Geral de Jacarepaguá,

The Hospital Geral de Realengo,

The Hospital Geral de Cândido Fontoura,

Hospital Geral de Nova

Private Clinics

Hospital So Lucas

Hospital Samaritano

Hospital Moinhos de Vento

Hospital Samaritano

Hospital Pró-Vida

Hospital So Vicente

Clinics

There are a variety of public and private clinics listed below

Centro de Sade de Botafogo

Centro de Sade de Copacabana

Centro de Sade de Ipanema

Centro de Sade do Méier, Clinica do Idoso

Clinica de Reabilitaço do Rio

Clinica da Famlia

Clinica de Cirurgias Plásticas.

Health Clinics

The city also has a multitude of health facilities, such the Centro de Salud de Tijuca, Botafogo, Copacabana, Méier, and Ipanema.

Specialty Facilities

Rio de Janeiro also has several specialized healthcare centers

Centro de Oncologia do Rio de Janeiro,

Centro de Reabilitaço Cardiovascular do Rio de Janeiro

Centro de Transplante de Medula ssea do Rio de Janeiro

Centro de Infertilidade do Rio de Janeiro

Centro de Obesidade do Rio de Janeiro

Centro de Psiquiatria do Rio de Janeiro.

Security safety

Rio de Janeiro has a reputation for being dangerous, especially at night and in the favelas (slums). Taking some simple safety measures, on the other hand, may help lessen the danger of crime.

Avoiding exhibiting costly objects, remaining in well-lit places, not carrying big sums of cash, and not strolling alone at night are all examples. It's also a good idea to be alert of your surroundings, avoid using headphones or conversing on the phone, and keep a watch on your valuables.

Visitors should also be on the lookout for scams, such as those involving ATM, and should avoid wearing costly jewelry or other things that may attract attention. Therefore, it is usually preferable to travel in groups and to employ licensed and reputed transportation providers.

Security Capacity

Rio de Janeiro's security situation is complicated. The city has a long history of violence and crime, and although important measures have been made in recent years to address the issue, much more needs to be done.

To combat organized crime, the Brazilian government has adopted a number of security measures in the city, including the deployment of more police officers, military troops, and specialized units. In an attempt to curb violence, the city has also implemented a preventative policing policy, including community policing.

In addition to these measures, the government has initiated a variety of efforts to enhance Rio de Janeiro's security situation. These strategies include installing CCTV cameras in public places, increasing infrastructure investment, installing lights in public places, and developing a coordinated security network to fight organized crime.

Despite these efforts, Rio de Janeiro's security situation remains precarious. The city is plagued by high levels of crime and violence, with the number of killings increasing in recent years. Nonetheless, with further efforts and investments, the security situation in Rio de Janeiro has the potential to drastically improve in the next years.

Security facilities

Rio de Janeiro offers a variety of security services. Military police, civil police, federal police, the national guard, the fire department, the municipal guard, and the private security sector are all part of the security services.

The military police are in charge of public safety and law enforcement, whilst the civil police are in charge of criminal investigations. The federal police are in charge of guarding the country's borders and implementing federal laws.

For important events, the national guard is in charge of providing security. The fire department is in charge of dealing with fires and other emergencies.

The municipal guard is in charge of keeping the peace and providing protection in public locations. Private security services are provided by the private security industry to individuals, corporations, and organizations.

Chapter 12

FREE MAP APPS FOR LOCATIONS

The most crucial factor to consider while arranging a trip is convenience. Map applications have transformed the way we travel, bringing unparalleled simplicity, flexibility, and convenience to travellers.

Tourists may use map applications to navigate their way around a city or area. Tourists may use GPS to swiftly discover their location and determine the precise path they need to travel.

They may also acquire instructions to their target area, which makes it easy to locate the greatest spots to visit.

Map applications not only give valuable information like as opening hours, ratings, and contact information, but they also assist travelers in finding the greatest bargains and discounts when traveling. Some applications also enable travelers to pre-book hotels and restaurants, which is a great way to save money.

Tourists may also use map applications to get extensive information about the place they are visiting. Users may get full information on attractions and activities, as well as opening hours, pricing, and other pertinent data. Moreover, they may read evaluations from other people to ensure that the place is worth visiting.

Lastly, navigation applications can assist travelers in remaining safe while traveling. People can readily discover emergency assistance or the best path to their goal without getting lost or getting into difficulty.

Overall, map applications are a wonderful resource for travelers, giving convenience, flexibility, and security. They are an important element of every wise traveler's armory, assisting them in making the most of their trip.

Free Map Apps

Google Maps

Google Maps

Waze

CityMaps2Go

Offline Map and Guide to Rio de Janeiro

Cities Guides on TripAdvisor

Offline Sygic Travel Maps

Rio de Janeiro Offline Travel Guide City Plan

Tube Map of Rio de Janeiro

Map of Rio de Janeiro's Streets

How to used free map Apps

1. Get a free map app from the Apple App Store or Google Play.

2. Launch the app and choose your chosen location.

3. Choose the sort of map you want to see (satellite, 3D, topographical, etc.).

4. Zoom in and out to get a better look at the region you're looking for.

5. You may also look for addresses or places using the search box.

6. If you want instructions, enter your beginning and finishing locations to get them.

7. You may also bookmark your favorite destinations and build custom maps using the app's capabilities.

Map list in Rio de Janeiro

Christ the Redemption

Copacabana Beach

Sugarloaf Mountain

Ipanema Beach

National History Museum

Maracan Stadium

Tijuca National Park

Botanical Garden

Selarón's Steps

Sebastio   **Metropolitan**   **Cathedral**

Chapter 13

A WEEK SOLO TRIP & MEAL PLAN

A week solo journey overview

Day 1:

Begin your adventure in Rio de Janeiro by visiting the famous Copacabana beach. Spend the day soaking up the rays, people watching, and admiring the scenery.

Take a walk along the beach promenade and cool off in the water. Following a day of leisure, dine at one of the city's well-known steakhouses.

Day 2:

Take a tour of Rio's ancient city center today. Begin with the renowned Selarón Steps, then go to the Museum of Future and the National History Museum.

Once you've had your fill of museums, visit one of the city's numerous churches, such as the Candelária Church. In the afternoon, ride a cable car up Sugarloaf Mountain for panoramic views of the city.

Day 3:

This is the day to see Rio's well-known favelas. Enjoy a guided tour to learn more about the area's history and inhabitants. After your tour, visit the Botanical Gardens for a relaxing walk around the lovely grounds.

Day 4:

Rio de Janeiro, it's time to begin moving. Spend the day in Olympic Park, taking in the breathtaking scenery and participating in one of the various activities on offer. Following the thrill of the Olympic Park, wander down Ipanema Beach or enjoy a boat tour of Rio de Janeiro's harbor.

Day 5:

Visit the adjacent coastal town of Buzios for the day. Spend the day exploring the cobblestone alleys of the town, resting on the beach, and shopping for one-of-a-kind gifts.

Day 6:

Spend the day discovering the city's cultural highlights. Take a look around the Museum of Modern Art, the Teatro Municipal, and the National Library.

Day 7:

See Corcovado Mountain at the end of your week-long tour. Ride the train to the top for a beautiful perspective of the city. Following your stay, take one more walk around the city to take in all Rio de Janeiro has to offer.

A week Delicious & Nutritious Meal Plan

Day 1

Delicious fruit salad with yogurt and granola for breakfast

Fish stew with rice and steamed veggies for lunch

Feijoada (black bean and pork stew) with collard greens and farofa for dinner (manioc flour)

Day 2

Breakfast sandwich with egg and cheese with tomato and avocado

Lunch consists of beef kebabs with roasted potatoes and salad.

Moqueca de Peixe (fish stew with coconut milk and tomato) with rice and steamed veggies for dinner

Day 3

Acai bowl with fresh fruit for breakfast

Brazilian-style pizza with chorizo, olives, and cheese for lunch

Feijao Tropeiro (beans, pork, and collard greens) with white rice for dinner

Day 4

Grilled cheese sandwich with sliced tomatoes and avocado for breakfast

Grilled chicken with rice and beans for lunch

Moqueca de Camarao (shrimp stew with coconut milk and tomato) with white rice for dinner

Day 5

Breakfast: ham and cheese omelette

Feijoada (black bean and pig stew) with white rice for lunch

Grilled fish with steamed veggies and farofa for dinner (manioc flour)

Day 6

Avocado toast with scrambled eggs and fresh fruit for breakfast

Lunch: Creamy salmon with mashed potatoes and steamed veggies

Dinner: Brazilian-style meat and mozzarella lasagna

Day 7

Guava smoothie bowl with granola for breakfast

Stuffed peppers with rice, beans, and cheese for lunch

Quibebe (pumpkin and shrimp stew) with steamed veggies and white rice   for   dinner

Conclusion

Rio de Janeiro has something for everyone. There is definitely something for everyone, from the renowned Christ the Redeemer monument and Sugarloaf Mountain to the natural beauty of Copacabana Beach and Ipanema, and the pulsating nightlife of Lapa and Santa Teresa.

The city is also recognized for its superb gastronomy, which includes both traditional Brazilian meals like feijoada and acarajé and inventive fusion dishes. Rio also boasts a thriving cultural scene, including internationally acclaimed music, art, and dance.

While visiting Rio, make sure to take in the breathtaking views of the city from Corcovado and Po de Açar, as well as spend time exploring the bustling areas of Copacabana, Ipanema, and Lapa.

Rio de Janeiro is a city unlike any other, with a one-of-a-kind blend of beauty, culture, and nightlife that makes it a must-see trip. So don't put it off any longer; go discover Rio de Janeiro now!

Printed in Great Britain
by Amazon

20862378R00078